I0209374

Thomas Paine, Melchior Steiner

Letter Addressed to the Abbé Raynal, on the Affairs of

North-America

Thomas Paine, Melchior Steiner

Letter Addressed to the Abbé Raynal, on the Affairs of North-America

ISBN/EAN: 9783337105808

Printed in Europe, USA, Canada, Australia, Japan

Cover: Foto ©ninafisch / pixelio.de

More available books at **www.hansebooks.com**

LETTER

ADDRESSED TO THE

ABBE RAYNAL

ON THE

AFFAIRS of *North-America*,

IN WHICH

The Miſtakes in the Abbe's Account

OF THE

REVOLUTION OF AMERICA

ARE CORRECTED AND CLEARED UP.

By THOMAS PAINE, M. A.

of the Univerſity of Pennſylvania, and Author of the Pamphlet
and other Publications, entitled, "COMMON SENSE."

PHILADELPHIA:

Printed by MELCHIOR STEINER, in Race-ſtreet,
near Third-ſtreet.

And Sold by ROBERT AITKEN, Bookſeller, in Market-
ſtreet, three Doors above the Coffee-Houſe.

M,DCC,LXXXII.

INTRODUCTION.

A LONDON tranflation of an original work in French, by the Abbe Raynal, which treats of the Revolution of North-America, having been reprinted in Philadelphia and other parts of the continent, and as the diftance at which the Abbe is placed from the American theatre of war and politics, has occafioned him to miftake feveral facts, or, mifconceive the caufes or principles by which they were produced ; the following tract, therefore, is publifhed with a view to rectify them, and prevent even accidental errors intermixing with hiftory, under the fanction of time and filence.

THE editor of the London edition has entitled it, "*The Revolution of America*, by the ABBE RAYNAL," and the American printers have followed the example. But I have underftood, and I believe my information juft, that the piece, which is more properly reflections on the revolution, was unfairly purloined from the printer which the Abbe employed, or from the manufcript copy, and is only part of a larger work then in the prefs, or preparing for it. The perfon who procured it appears to have been an Englifhman, and though in an advertifement prefixt to the London edition, he has endeavoured to glofs over the embezzlement with profeffions of patriotifm, and to

soften

soften it with high encomiums on the author, yet the action, in any view, in which it can be placed, is illiberal and unpardonable.

" In the course of his travels," says he, " the translator
" happily succeeded in obtaining a copy of this exquisite
" little piece, which has not yet made its appearance from
" any press. He publishes a French edition, in favour of
" those who will feel its eloquent reasoning more forcibly
" in its native language, at the same time with the fol-
" lowing translation of it; in which he has been desirous,
" perhaps in vain, that all the warmth, the grace, the
" strength, the dignity of the original, should not be lost.
" And he flatters himself, that the indulgence of the illu-
" strious historian will not be wanting to a man, who,
" of his own motion, has taken the liberty to give this
" composition to the public, only from a strong persua-
" sion, that its momentous argument will be useful, in
" a critical conjuncture, to that country which he loves
" with an ardour, that can be exceeded only by the
" nobler flame, which burns in the bosom of the philan-
" thropic author, for the freedom and happiness of all
" the countries upon earth."

This plausibility of setting off a dishonorable action, may pass for patriotism, and sound principles with those who do not enter into its demerits, and whose interest is not injured nor their happiness affected thereby. But it is more than probable, notwithstanding the declarations it contains, that the copy was obtained for the sake of profiting by the sale of a new and popular work, and that the professions are but a garb to the fraud.

It may with propriety be remarked, that in all countries where literature is protected, and it never can flourish where it is not, the works of an author are his legal property; and to treat letters in any other light than this, is to banish them from the country or strangle them in the birth.----The embezzlement from the Abbe Raynal, was, it is true, committed by one country upon another, and therefore shows no defect in the laws of either. But it is nevertheless a breach of civil manners and literary justice; neither can it be any apology, that because the

countries

countries are at war, literature fhall be entitled to depre-dation. *

But the foreftalling the Abbe's publication by London editions, both in French and Englifh, and thereby hot only defrauding him and throwing an expenfive publication on his hands by anticipating the fale, are only the fmaller injuries which fuch conduct may occafion. A man's opinions, whether written or in thought, are his own until he pleafes to publifh them himfelf; and it is adding cruelty to injuftice, to make him the author of what future reflection; or better information, might occafion him to fupprefs or amend. There are declarations and fentiments in the Abbe's piece, which, for my own part, I did not expect to find, and fuch as himfelf, on a revifal, might have feen occafion to change; but the anticipated piracy effectually prevented him the opportunity, and precipitated him into difficulties, which, had it not been for fuch ungenerous fraud, might not have happened.

This mode of making an author appear before his time, will appear ftill more ungenerous, when we confider how exceedingly few men there are in any country, who can at once, and without the aid of reflection and revifal, combine warm paffions with a cool temper, and the full expanfion of imagination with the natural and neceffary gravity of judgment, fo as to be rightly balanced within themfelves, and to make a reader feel, fancy, and underftand juftly at the fame time. To call three powers of the

A 2

---

* *The ftate of literature in America muft one day become a fubject of legiflative confideration. Hitherto it hath been a difintereftecl volunteer in the fervice of the revolution, and no man thought of profits: but when peace fhall give time and opportunity for ftudy, the country will deprive itfelf of the honor and fervice of letters and the improvement of fcience, unlefs fufficient laws are made to prevent depredations on literary property.--- It is well worth remarking, that Ruffia, who but a few years ago, was fcarcely known in Europe, owes a large fhare of her prefent greatnefs to the clofe attention fhe has paid, and the wife encouragement fhe has given, to every branch of fcience and learning; and we have almoft the fame inftance in France, in the reign of Lewis the XIV.*

the mind into action at once, in a manner that neither shall interrupt, and that each shall aid and vigorate the other, is a talent very rarely possessed.

It often happens that the weight of an argument is lost by the wit of setting it off; or the judgment disordered by an intemperate irritation of the passions : yet a certain degree of animation must be felt by the writer, and raised in the reader, in order to interest the attention ; and a sufficient scope given to the imagination, to enable it to create in the mind a sight of the persons, characters and circumstances of the subject; for without these the judgment will feel little or no excitement to office, and its determinations will be cold, sluggish, and imperfect. But if either or both of the two former are raised too high, or heated to much, the judgment will be jostled from its feat, and the whole matter, however important in itself, will diminish into a pantomime of the mind, in which we create images that promote no other purpose than amusement.

The Abbe's writings bear evident marks of that extension and rapidness of thinking and quickness of sensation, which of all others require revisal, and the more particularly so, when applied to the living characters of nations or individuals in a state of war. The least misinformation or misconception leads to some wrong conclusion, and an error believed becomes the progenitor of others.---And as the Abbe has suffered some inconveniencies in France by mistating certain circumstances of the war, and the characters of the parties therein, it becomes some apology for him that those errors were precipitated into the world by the avarice of an ungenerous enemy.

LETTER

L E T T E R

ADDRESSED TO THE

ABBE RAYNAL

ON THE AFFAIRS OF

NORTH-AMERICA.

TO an author of such distinguished reputation as the Abbe Raynal, it might very well become me to apologize for the present undertaking; but as *to be right* is the first wish of philosophy, and the first principle of history, he will, I presume, accept from me a declaration of my motives, which are those of doing justice, in preference to any complimental apology, I might otherwise make.-----The Abbe, in the course of his work, has, in some instances, extolled without a reason, and wounded without a cause. He has given fame where it was not deserved, and withheld it where it was justly due; and appears to be so frequently in and out of temper with

his

his fubjects and parties, that few or none of them are decifively and uniformly marked.

It is yet too foon to write the hiftory of the revolution, and whoever attempts it precipitately, will unavoidably miftake characters and circumftances, and involve himfelf in error and difficulty. Things like men are feldom underftood rightly at firft fight. But the Abbe is wrong even in the foundation of his work; that is, he has mifconceived and miftated the caufes which produced the rupture between England and her then colonies, and which led on, ftep by ftep, unftudied and uncontrived on the part of America, to a revolution, which has engaged the attention, and affected the intereft, of Europe.

To prove this, I fhall bring forward a paffage, which, though placed towards the latter part of the Abbe's work, is more intimately connected with the beginning; and in which, fpeaking of the original caufe of the difpute, he declares himfelf in the following manner---

"None," fays he, "of thofe energetic caufes, which
"have produced fo many revolutions upon the globe,
"exifted in North-America. Neither religion nor laws
"had there been outraged. The blood of martyrs or
"patriots had not there ftreamed from fcaffolds. Morals
"had not there been infulted. Manners, cuftoms, ha-
"bits, no object dear to nations, had there been the fport
"of ridicule. Arbitrary power had not there torn any
"inhabitant from the arms of his family and his friends,
"to drag him to a dreary dungeon. Public order had
"not been there inverted. The principles of adminiftra-
"tion had not been changed there; and the maxims of
"govern-

" government had there always remained the fame. The
" whole queftion was reduced to the knowing whether
" the mother country had, or had not a right to lay, di-
" rectly or indirectly, a flight tax upon the colonies."

On this extraordinary paffage, it may not be improper,
in general terms, to remark, that none can feel like thofe
who fuffer; and that for a man to be a competent judge
of the provocative, or as the Abbe ftiles them, the energetic caufes of the revolution, he muft have refided in
America.

The Abbe in faying that the feveral particulars he has
enumerated, did not exift in America, and neglecting to
point out the particular period, in which he means they
did not exift, reduces thereby his declaration to a nullity,
by taking away all meaning from the paffage.

They did not exift in 1763, and they all exifted before 1776; confequently as there was a time when they
did not, and another, when they *did* exift, the *time when*
conftitutes the effence of the fact, and not to give it, is
to withhold the only evidence, which proves the declaration right or wrong, and on which it muft ftand or fall.
But the declaration, as it now appears, unaccompanied
by time, has an effect in holding out to the world, that
there was no real caufe for the revolution, becaufe it
denies the exiftence of all thofe caufes, which are fuppofed
to be juftifiable and which the Abbe ftiles energetic.

I confefs myfelf exceedingly at a lofs to find out the
time to which the Abbe alludes; becaufe, in another part
of the work, in fpeaking of the ftamp act, which was

paffed

paffed in 1764, he ftiles it " An *ufurpation* of the Americans *moft precious and facred rights*." Confequently he here admits the moft energetic of all caufes, that is, *an ufurpation of their moft precious and facred rights*, to have exifted in America twelve years before the declaration of independence, and ten years before the breaking out of hoftilities.---The time, therefore, in which the paragraph is true, muft be antecedent to the ftamp act, but as at that time there was no revolution nor any idea of one, it confequently applies without a meaning; and as it cannot, on the Abbe's own principle, be applied to any time *after* the ftamp act, it is therefore a wandering folitary paragraph connected with nothing and at variance with every thing.

THE ftamp act, it is true, was repealed in two years after it was paffed, but it was immediately followed by one of infinitely more mifchievous magnitude, I mean the declaratory act, which afferted the right, as it was ftiled, of the Britifh Parliament, "*to bind America in all cafes whatfoever.*"

IF then the ftamp act was an ufurpation of the Americans moft precious and facred rights, the declaratory act left them no right at all; and contained the full grown feeds of the moft defpotic government ever exercifed in the world. It placed America not only in the loweft, but in the bafeft ftate of vaffalage; becaufe it demanded an unconditional fubmiffion in every thing, or as the act expreffes it, *in all cafes whatfoever :* And what renders this act the more offenfive, is, that it appears to have been paffed as an act of mercy; truly then may it be faid, that *the tender mercies of the wicked are cruel.*

ALL

ALL the original charters from the Crown of England, under the faith of which, the adventurers from the old world fettled in the new, were by this act difplaced from their foundations; becaufe, contrary to the nature of them, which was that of a compact, they were now made fubject to repeal or alteration at the meer will of one party only. The whole condition of America was thus put into the hands of the Parliament or the Miniftry, without leaving to her the leaft right in any cafe whatfoever.

THERE is no defpotifm to which this iniquitous law did not extend; and tho' it might have been convenient in the execution of it, to have confulted manners and habits, the principle of the act made all tyranny legal. It ftopt nowhere. It went to every thing. It took in with it the whole life of a man, or, if I may fo exprefs it, an eternity of circumftances. It is the nature of law to require obedience, but this demanded fervitude; and the condition of an American, under the operation of it, was not that of a fubject, but a vaffal. Tyranny has often been eftablifhed *without* law and fometimes *againft* it, but the hiftory of mankind does not produce another inftance, in which it has been eftablifhed *by* law. It is an audacious outrage upon civil government, and cannot be too much expofed, in order to be fufficiently detefted.

NEITHER could it be faid after this, that the legiflature of that country any longer made laws for this, but that it gave out commands; for wherein differed an act of Parliament conftructed on this principle, and operating in this manner, over an unreprefented people, from the orders of a military eftablifhment.

THE

THE Parliament of England, with refpect to America, was not feptennial but *perpetual*. It appeared to the latter a body always in being. Its election or its expiration were to her the fame as if its members fucceeded by inheritance, or went out by death, or lived for ever, or were appointed to it as a matter of office. Therefore, for the people of England to have any juft conception of the mind of America, refpecting this extraordinary act, they muft fuppofe all election and expiration in that country to ceafe for ever, and the prefent Parliament, its heirs, &c. to be perpetual; in this cafe, I afk, what would the moft clamorous of them think, were an act to be paffed, declaring the right of *fuch a Parliament* to bind *them* in all cafes whatfoever? For this word *whatfoever* would go as effectually to their *Magna Charta*, *Bill of Rights*, *Trial by Juries*, &c. as it went to the charters and forms of government in America.

I am perfuaded, that the Gentleman to whom I addrefs thefe remarks, will not, after the paffing this act, fay, " That the *principles* of adminiftration had not been " *changed* in America, and that the maxims of govern- " ment had there been *always the fame*." For here is, in principle, a total overthrow of the whole; and not a fubverfion only, but an annihilation of the foundation of liberty, and abfolute domination eftablifhed in its ftead.

THE Abbe likewife ftates the cafe exceedingly wrong and injurioufly, when he fays, " that *the whole* queftion " was reduced to the knowing whether the mother coun- " try had, or had not, a right to lay, directly or indi- " rectly, a *flight* tax upon the colonies."---This was

not

not the whole of the queſtion ; neither was the *quantity* of the tax the objeƈt, either to the Miniſtry or to the Americans. It was the principle, of which the tax made but a part, and the quantity ſtill leſs, that formed the ground on which America oppoſed.

THE tax on tea, which is the tax here alluded to, was neither more or leſs than an experiment to eſtabliſh the practice of the declaratory law upon ; modelled into the more faſhionable phraſe *of the univerſal ſupremacy of Parliament.* For until this time the declaratory law had lain dormant, and the framers of it had contented themſelves with barely declaring an opinion.

THEREFORE the *whole* queſtion with America, in the opening of the diſpute, was, ſhall we be bound in all caſes whatſoever by the Britiſh parliament, or ſhall we not ? For ſubmiſſion to the tea or tax aƈt implied an acknowledgment of the declaratory aƈt, or, in other words, of the univerſal ſupremacy of Parliament, which, as they never intended to do, it was neceſſary they ſhould oppoſe it, in its firſt ſtage of execution.

IT is probable, the Abbe has been led into this miſtake by peruſing detached pieces in ſome of the American News-Papers ; for in a caſe, where all were intereſted, every one had a right to give his opinion ; and there were many, who with the beſt intentions, did not chuſe the beſt, nor indeed the true ground, to defend their cauſe upon. They felt themſelves right by a general impulſe, without being able to ſeparate, analyze, and arrange the parts.

I am ſomewhat unwilling to examine too minutely into

the

the whole of this extraordinary paſſage of the Abbe, leſt I ſhould appear to treat it with ſeverity; otherwiſe I could ſhow that not a ſingle declaration is juſtly founded : For inſtance, the reviving an obſolete act of the reign of Henry the eighth, and fitting it to the Americans, by authority of which they were to be ſeized and brought from America to England, and there impriſoned and tried for any ſuppoſed offences, was, in the worſt ſenſe of the words, *to tear them, by the arbitrary power of Parliament, from the arms of their families and friends, and drag them not only to dreary but diſtant dungeons.* Yet this act was contrived ſome years before the breaking out of hoſtilities. And again, though the blood of martyrs and patriots had not ſtreamed on the ſcaffolds, it ſtreamed in the ſtreets, in the maſſacre of the inhabitants of Boſton, by the Britiſh ſoldiery in the year 1770.

HAD the Abbe ſaid that the cauſes which produced the revolution in America were originally *different* from thoſe which produced revolutions in other parts of the globe, he had been right. Here the value and quality of liberty, the nature of government, and the dignity of man, were known and underſtood, and the attachment of the Americans to theſe principles produced the revolution as a natural and almoſt unavoidable conſequence. They had no particular family to ſet up or pull down. Nothing of perſonality was incorporated with their cauſe. They ſtarted even-handed with each other, and went no faſter into the ſeveral ſtages of it, than they were driven by the unrelenting and imperious conduct of Britain. Nay, in the laſt act, the declaration of independence, they had nearly been too late ; for had it not been declared at the exact time it was, I ſee no period in their affairs ſince, in

which

which it could have been declared with the fame effect, and probably not at all.

But the object being formed before the reverfe of fortune took place, that is, before the operations of the gloomy campaign of 1776, their honor, their intereft, their every thing called loudly on them to maintain it; and that glow of thought and energy of heart, which even a diftant profpect of independence infpires, gave confidence to their hopes and refolution to their conduct, which a ftate of dependence could never have reached. They looked forward to happier days and fcenes of reft, and qualified the hardfhips of the campaign by contemplating the eftablifhment of their new born fyftem.

If on the other hand we take a review of what part Britain has acted, we fhall find every thing which ought to make a nation blufh. The moft vulgar abufe, accompanied by that fpecies of haughtinefs, which diftinguifhes the hero of a mob from the character of a gentleman ; it was equally as much from her manners as from her injuftice that fhe loft the colonies. By the latter fhe provoked their principles, by the former fhe wore out their temper; and it ought to be held out as an example to the world, to fhow, how neceffary it is to conduct the bufinefs of government with civility. In fhort, other revolutions may have originated in caprice or generated in ambition ; but here, the moft unoffending humility was tortured into rage, and the infancy of exiftence made to weep.

A union fo extenfive, continued and determined, fuffering with patience and never in defpair, could not have been produced by common caufes. It muft be fomething
capable

capable of reaching the whole foul of man and arming it with perpetual energy. In vain is it to look for precedents among the revolutions of former ages, to find out, by comparifon, the caufes of this. The fpring, the progrefs, the objeCt, the confequences, nay, the men, their habits of thinking, and all the circumftances of the country are different. Thofe of other nations are, in general, little more than the hiftory of their quarrels. They are marked by no important charaCter in the annals of events; mixt in the mafs of general matters they occupy but a common page; and while the chief of the fuccefsful partizans ftept into power, the plundered multitude fat down and forrowed. Few, very few of them are accompanied with reformation, either in government or manners; many of them with the moft confummate profligacy. Triumph on the one fide and mifery on the other were the only events. Pains, punifhments, torture, and death were made the bufinefs of mankind, until compaffion, the faireft affociate of the heart, was driven from its place, and the eye, accuftomed to continual cruelty, could behold it without offence.

But as the principles of the prefent revolution differed from thofe which preceded it, fo likewife has the conduCt of America both in government and war. Neither the foul finger of difgrace nor the bloody hand of vengeance has hitherto put a blot upon her fame. Her viCtories have received luftre from a greatnefs of lenity; and her laws been permitted to flumber, where they might juftly have awakened to punifh. War, fo much the trade of the world, has here been only the bufinefs of neceffity; and when the neceffity fhall ceafe, her very enemies muft con-

fefs,

fefs, that as fhe drew the fword in her juft defence, fhe ufed it without cruelty and fheathed it without revenge.

As it is not my defign to extend thefe remarks to a hiftory, I fhall now take my leave of this paffage of the Abbe, with an obfervation, which until fomething unfolds itfelf to convince me otherwife, I cannot avoid believing to be true;---which is, that it was the fixt determination of the Britifh cabinet to quarrel with America at all events.

They (the members who compofe the cabinet) had no doubt of fuccefs, if they could once bring it to the iffue of a battle; and they expected from a conqueft, what they could neither propofe with decency, nor hope for by negociation. The charters and conftitutions of the colonies were become to them matters of offence, and their rapid progrefs in property and population were difguftingly beheld as the growing and natural means of independence. They faw no way to retain them long but by reducing them in time. A conqueft would at once have made them both lords and landlords; and put them in poffeffion both of the revenue and the rental. The whole trouble of government would have ceafed in a victory, and a final end been put to remonftrance and debate. The experience of the ftamp act had taught them how to quarrel with the advantages of cover and convenience, and they had nothing to do but to renew the fcene, and put contention into motion. They hoped for a rebellion, and they made one. They expected a declaration of independence, and they were not difappointed. But after this, they looked for victory, and they obtained a defeat.

If

If this be taken as the generating cauſe of the conteſt, then is every part of the conduct of the Britiſh Miniſtry conſiſtent from the commencement of the diſpute, until the ſigning the treaty of Paris, after which, conqueſt becoming doubtful, they retreated to negociation, and were again defeated.

Tho' the Abbe poſſeſſes and diſplays great powers of genius, and is a maſter of ſtile and language, he ſeems not to pay equal attention to the office of an hiſtorian. His facts are coldly and carcleſsly ſtated. They neither inform the reader nor intereſt him. Many of them are erroneous, and moſt of them defective and obſcure. It is undoubtedly both an ornament and a uſeful addition to hiſtory to accompany it with maxims and reflections. They afford likewiſe an agreeable change to the ſtile and a more diverſified manner of expreſſion ; but it is abſolutely neceſſary that the root from whence they ſpring, or the foundations on which they are raiſed, ſhould be well attended to, which in this work they are not. The Abbe haſtens through his narrations as if he was glad to get from them, that he may enter the more copious field of eloquence and imagination.

The actions of Trenton and Princeton in New-Jerſey, in December 1776, and January following, on which the fate of America ſtood for a while trembling on the point of ſuſpence, and from which the moſt important conſequences followed, are compriſed within a ſingle paragraph faintly conceived, and barren of character, circumſtance and diſcription.

"On the 25th of December," ſays the Abbe, "they
(the

" (the Americans) croffed the Delaware, and fell *acci-*
" *dentally* upon Trenton, which was occupied by fifteen
" hundred of the twelve thoufand Heffians, fold in fo
" bafe a manner by their avaricious mafter, to the King
" of Great Britain. This corps was *maffacred*, taken,
" or difperfed. Eight days after, three Englifh regiments
" were in like manner driven from Princeton, but after
" having better fupported their reputation than the foreign
" troops in their pay."

THIS is all the account which is given of thefe moft
interefting events. The Abbe has preceded them by two
or three pages on the military operations of both armies,
from the time of General Howe arriving before New-
York from Hallifax, and the vaft reinforcements of Britifh
and foreign troops with Lord Howe from England. But
in thefe, there is fo much miftake, and fo many omif-
fions, that, to fet them right, muft be the bufinefs of hiftory and not of a letter. The action of Long-Ifland is
but barely hinted at, and the operations at the White
Plains wholly omitted : as are likewife the attack and lofs
of fort Wafhington, with a garrifon of about two thoufand
five hundred men, and the precipitate evacuation of Fort
Lee, in confequence thereof; which loffes were in a great
meafure the caufe of the retreat through the Jerfies to the
Delaware, a diftance of about ninety miles. Neither is
the manner of the retreat defcribed, which, from the feafon
of the year, the nature of the country, the nearnefs of the
two armies, (fometimes within fight and fhot of each
other for fuch a length of way) the rear of the one employed in pulling down bridges, and the van of the other
in building them up, muft neceffarily be accompanied with
many interefting circumftances.

C   IT

It was a period of diftrefles. A crifis rather of danger than of hope. There is no defcription can do it juftice; and even the actors in it, looking back upon the fcene, are furprifed how they got through; and at a lofs to account for thofe powers of the mind and fprings of animation, by which they withftood the force of accumulated misfortune.

It was expected, that the time for which the army was inlifted, would carry the campaign fo far into the winter, that the feverity of the feafon, and the confequent condition of the roads, would prevent any material operation of the enemy, until the new army could be raifed for the next year. And I mention it, as a matter worthy of attention, by all future hiftorians, that the movements of the American army, until the attack upon the Heffian poft at Trenton, the 26th of December, are to be confidered as operating to effect no other principal purpofe than delay, and to wear away the campaign under all the difadvantages of an unequal force, with as little misfortune as poffible.

But the lofs of the garrifon at fort Wafhington on the 16th of November, and the expiration of the time of a confiderable part of the army, fo early as the 30th of the fame month, and which were to be followed by almoft daily expirations afterwards, made retreat the only final expedient. To thefe circumftances may be added the forlorn and deftitute condition of the few that remained; for the garrifon of Fort Lee, which compofed almoft the whole of the retreat, had been obliged to abandon it fo inftantaneoufly, that every article of ftores and baggage was left behind, and in this deftitute condition, without tent or blanket, and without any other utenfils to drefs their

provifion,

provifion than what they procured by the way, they performed a march of about ninety miles, and had the addrefs
and management to prolong it to the fpace of nineteen days.

By this unexpected or rather unthought of turn of affairs, the country was in an inftant furprifed into confufion, and found an enemy within its bowels, without an
army to oppofe him. There were no fuccours to be had,
but from the free-will offering of the inhabitants. All was
choice and every man reafoned for himfelf.

It was in this fituation of affairs, equally calculated
to confound or to infpire, that the gentleman, the mer-
chant, the farmer, the tradefman and the labourer mutually turned from all the conveniencies of home, to per-
form the duties of private foldiers and undergo the feveri-
ties of a winter campaign. The delay, fo judicioufly
contrived on the retreat, afforded time for the volunteer
reinforcements to join General Wafhington on the Delaware.

The Abbe is likewife wrong in faying, that the American army fell *accidentally* on Trenton. It was the very
object for which General Wafhington croffed the Delaware in the dead of the night and in the midft of fnow,
ftorms, and ice; and which he immediately recroffed with
his prifoners, as foon as he had accomplifhed his purpofe.
Neither was the intended enterprife a fecret to the enemy,
information having been fent of it by letter, from a Britifh Officer at Princeton to Colonel Rolle, who com-
manded the Heffians at Trenton, which letter was afterwards found by the Americans. Neverthelefs the poft
was completely furprifed. A fmall circumftance, which

had

had the appearance of miſtake on the part of the Americans, led to a more capital and real miſtake on the part
of Rolle.

THE caſe was this. A detachment of twenty or thirty
Americans had been ſent acroſs the river from a poſt, a few
miles above, by an Officer unacquainted with the intended
attack ; theſe were met by a body of Heſſians on the night,
to which the information pointed, which was Chriſtmas
night, and repulſed. Nothing further appearing, and the
Heſſians, miſtaking this for the advanced party, ſuppoſed
the enterpriſe diſconcerted, which at that time was not
began, and under this idea, returned to their quarters ; ſo
that, what might have raiſed an alarm, and brought the
Americans into an ambuſcade, ſerved to take off the force
of an information and promote the ſucceſs of the enterpriſe. Soon after day light General Waſhington entered
the town, and after a little oppoſition, made himſelf maſter
of it, with upwards of nine hundred priſoners.

THIS combination of equivocal circumſtances, falling
within what the Abbe ſtiles *" the wide empire of chance,"*
would have afforded a fine field for thought, and I wiſh,
for the ſake of that elegance of reflection he is ſo capable
of uſing, that he had known it.

BUT the action at Princeton was accompanied by a ſtill
greater embaraſment of matters, and followed by more
extraordinary conſequences. The Americans, by a happy ſtroke of generalſhip, in this inſtance, not only de-
ranged and defeated all the plans of the Britiſh, in the
intended moment of execution, but drew from their poſts
the enemy they were not able to drive, and obliged them

to

to clofe the campaign. As the circumftance is a curiofity in war and not well underftood in Europe, I fhall, as concifely as I can, relate the principal parts; they may ferve to prevent future hiftorians from error, and recover from forgetfulnefs a fcene of magnificent fortitude.

IMMEDIATELY after the furprize of the Heffians at Trenton, General Wafhington recroffed the Delaware, which at this place is about three quarters of a mile over, and reaffumed his former poft on the Pennfylvania fide. Trenton remained unoccupied, and the enemy were pofted at Princeton, twelve miles diftant, on the road towards New-York. The weather was now growing very fevere, and as there were very few houfes near the fhore where General Wafhington had taken his ftation, the greateft part of his army remained out in the woods and fields. Thefe, with fome other circumftances, induced the recroffing the Delaware and taking poffeffion of Trenton. It was undoubtedly a bold adventure, and carried with it the appearance of defiance, efpecially when we confider the panic ftruck condition of the enemy on the lofs of the Heffian poft. But in order to give a juft idea of the affair, it is neceffary, I fhould defcribe the place.

TRENTON is fituated on a rifing ground, about three quarters of a mile diftant from the Delaware, on the eaftern or Jerfey fide; and is cut into two divifions by a fmall creek or rivulet, fufficient to turn a mill which is on it, after which it empties itfelf at nearly right angles into the Delaware. The upper divifion which is to the north eaft, contains about feventy or eighty houfes, and the lower about forty or fifty. The ground on each fide this creek, and on which the houfes are, is likewife rifing, and the

two

two divifions prefent an agreeable profpect to each other, with the creek between, on which there is a fmall ftone bridge of one arch.

Scarcely had General Wafhington taken poft here, and before the feveral parties of militia, out on detachments, or on their way, could be collected, than the Britifh, leaving behind them a ftrong garrifon at Princeton, marched fuddenly and entered Trenton at the upper or north eaft quarter. A party of the Americans fkirmifhed with the advanced party of the Britifh, to afford time for removing the ftores and baggage, and withdrawing over the bridge.

In a little time the Britifh had poffeffion of one half of the town, General Wafhington of the other, and the creek only feparated the two armies. Nothing could be a more critical fituation than this, and if ever the fate of America depended on the event of a day, it was now. The Delaware was filling faft with large fheets of driving ice and was impaffable, fo that no retreat into Pennfylvania could be effected, neither is it poffible, in the face of an enemy, to pafs a river of fuch extent. The roads were broken and rugged with the froft, and the main road was occupied by the enemy.

About four o'clock a party of the Britifh approached the bridge, with a defign to gain it, but were repulfed. They made no more attempts, though the creek itfelf is pafsable any where between the bridge and the Delaware. It runs in a rugged natural made ditch, over which a perfon may pafs with little difficulty, the ftream being rapid and fhallow. Evening was now coming on, and the Britifh, believing they had all the advantages they could wifh for,

and

and that they could ufe them when they pleafed, difcon-
tinued all further operations, and held themfelves prepared
to make the attack next morning.

BUT the next morning produced a fcene, as elegant as
it was unexpected. The Britifh were under arms and
ready to march to action, when one of their light-horfe
from Princeton came furioufly down the ftreet, with an
account, that General Wafhington had that morning at-
tacked and carried the Britifh poft at that place, and was
proceeding on to feize the magazine at Brunfwick; on
which the Britifh, who were then on the point of making an
affault on the evacuated camp of the Americans, wheeled
about, and in a fit of confternation marched for Princeton.

THIS retreat is one of thofe extraordinary circumftances, that in future ages may probably pafs for fable.
For it will with difficulty be believed, that two armies, on
which fuch important confequences depended, fhould be
crouded into fo fmall a fpace as Trenton, and that the
one, on the eve of an engagement, when every ear is fuppofed to be open, and every watchfulnefs employed, fhould
move completely from the ground, with all its ftores, baggage, and artillery, unknown and even unfufpected by
the other. And fo entirely were the Britifh deceived, that
when they heard the report of the cannon and fmall arms
at Princeton, they fuppofed it to be thunder, though in
the depth of winter.

General Wafhington, the better to cover and difguife
his retreat from Trenton, had ordered a line of fires to be
lighted up in front of his camp. Thefe not only ferved
to give an appearance of going to reft, and continuing

that

that deception, but they effectually concealed from the British whatever was acting behind them, for flame can no more be seen through than a wall, and in this situation, it may with some propriety be said, they became a pillar of fire to the one army, and a pillar of a cloud to the other : after this, by a circuitous march of about eighteen miles, the Americans reached Princeton early in the morning.

THE number of prisoners taken were between two and three hundred, with which General Washington immediately set off. The van of the British army from Trenton entered Princeton about an hour after the Americans had left it, who continuing their march for the remainder of the day, arrived in the evening at a convenient situation, wide of the main road to Brunfwick, and about sixteen miles distant from Princeton.----But so wearied and exhausted were they, with the continual and unabated service and fatigue of two days and a night, from action to action, without shelter and almost without refreshment, that the bare and frozen ground, with no other covering than the sky, became to them a place of comfortable rest. By these two events, and with but little comparative force to accomplish them, the Americans closed with advantages a campaign, which, but a few days before, threatened the country with destruction. The British army, apprehensive for the safety of their magazines at Brunfwick, eighteen miles distant, marched immediately for that place, where they arrived late in the evening, and from which they made no attempts to move, for nearly five months.

HAVING thus stated the principal outlines of these two most interesting actions, I shall now quit them, to put the

Abbe

Abbe right in his miſtated account of the debt and paper money of America, wherein, ſpeaking of theſe matters, he ſays,

" Theſe ideal riches were rejected. The more the
" multiplication of them was urged by want, the greater
" did their depreciation grow. The Congreſs was indig-
" nant at the affronts given to its money, and declared all
" thoſe to be traitors to their country who ſhould not re-
" ceive it as they would have received gold itſelf.

" Did not this body know, that prepoſſeſſions are no
" more to be controled than feelings are? Did it not per-
" ceive, that in the preſent criſis every rational man would
" be afraid of expoſing his fortune? Did it not ſee, that
" at the beginning of a republic it permitted to itſelf the
" exerciſe of ſuch acts of deſpotiſm as are unknown even
" in the countries which are moulded to, and become fa-
" miliar with, ſervitude and oppreſſion? Could it pretend
" that it did not puniſh a want of confidence with the
" pains which would have been ſcarcely merited by revolt
" and treaſon? Of all this was the Congreſs well aware.
" But it had no choice of means. Its deſpiſed and deſpi-
" cable ſcraps of paper were actually thirty times below
" their original value, when more of them were ordered
" to be made. On the 13th of September, 1779, there
" was of this paper money, amongſt the public, to the
" amount of £35,544,155. The ſtate owed moreover
" £8,385,356, without reckoning the particular debts of
" ſingle provinces."

In the above recited paſſages the Abbe ſpeaks as if the United States had contracted a debt of upwards of forty

millions

millions pounds sterling, besides the debts of individual
States. After which, speaking of foreign trade with America, he says, that " those countries in Europe, which are
" truly commercial ones, knowing that North-America
" had been reduced to contract debts at the epoch of even
" her greatest prosperity, wisely thought, that, in her pre-
" sent distress, she would be able to pay but very little,
" for what might be carried to her."

I know it must be extremely difficult to make foreign-
ers understand the nature and circumstances of our paper
money, because there are natives, who do not understand
it themselves. But with us its fate is now determined.
Common consent has configned it to rest with that kind
of regard, which the long service of inanimate things in-
sensibly obtains from mankind. Every stone in the bridge,
that has carried us over, seems to have a claim upon our
esteem. But this was a corner stone, and its usefulness
cannot be forgotten. There is something in a grateful
mind, which extents itself even to things that can neither
be benefited by regard, nor suffer by neglect;---But so it
is; and almost every man is sensible of the effect.

BUT to return. The paper money, though issued from
Congress under the name of dollars, did not come from
that body always at that value. Those which were issued the first year, were equal to gold and silver. The
second year less, the third still less, and so on, for nearly
the space of five years; at the end of which, I imagine,
that the whole value, at which Congress might pay away
the several emissions, taking them together, was about
ten or twelve millions pounds sterling.

Now

Now as it would have taken ten or twelve millions fterling of taxes, to carry on the war for five years, and, as while this money was iffuing and likewife depreciating down to nothing, there were none, or few valuable taxes paid; confequently the event to the public was the fame, whether they funk ten or twelve millions of expended money, by depreciation, or paid ten or twelve millions by taxation; for as they did not do both, and chofe to do one, the matter which, in a general view, was indifferent. And therefore, what the Abbe fuppofes to be a debt, has now no exiftence; it having been paid, by every body confenting, to reduce at his own expence, from the value of the bills continually paffing among themfelves, a fum, equal to nearly what the expence of the war was for five years.

AGAIN. The paper money having now ceafed, and the depreciation with it, and gold and filver fupplied its place, the war will now be carried on by taxation, which will draw from the public a confiderable lefs fum than what the depreciation drew; but as while they pay the former, they do not fuffer the latter, and as when they fuffered the latter, they did not pay the former, the thing will be nearly equal, with this moral advantage, that taxation occafions frugality and thought, and depreciation produced diffipation and carelefInefs.

AND again. If a man's portion of taxes comes to lefs than what he loft by the depreciation, it proves the alteration is in his favor. If it comes to more, and he is juftly affeffed, it fhows that he did not fuftain his proper fhare of depreciation, becaufe the one was as operatively his tax as the other.

IT

IT is true, that it never was intended, neither was it fore-
feen, that the debt contained in the paper currency fhould
fink itfelf in this manner; but as by the voluntary conduct of all and of every one it has arrived at this fate, the
debt is paid by thofe who owed it. Perhaps nothing was
ever fo univerfally the act of a country as this. Government had no hand in it. Every man depreciated his own
money by his own confent, for fuch was the effect, which
the raifing the nominal value of goods produced. But as
by fuch reduction he fuftained a lofs equal to what he
muft have paid to fink it by taxation, therefore the line
of juftice is to confider his lofs by the depreciation as his
tax for that time, and not to tax him when the war is
over, to make that money good in any other perfons
hands, which became nothing in his own.

AGAIN. The paper currency was iffued for the exprefs
purpofe of carrying on the war, It has performed that
fervice, without any other material charge to the public,
while it lafted. But to fuppofe, as fome did, that, at the
end of the war, it was to grow into gold or filver, or
become equal thereto, was to fuppofe that we were to
get two hundred millions of dollars by *going to war*, inftead of *paying* the coft of carrying it on.

BUT if any thing in the fituation of America, as to her
currency or her circumftances, yet remains not underftood,
then let it be remembered, that this war is the public's
war; the people's war; the country's war. It is *their*
independence that is to be fupported ; *their* property that
is to be fecured; *their* country that is to be faved. Here,
government, the army, and the people, are mutually
and reciprocally one. In other wars, kings may lofe their
thrones

thrones, and their dominions; but here, the lofs muft fall
on the majefty of the multitude, and the property they are
contending to fave. Every man being fenfible of this, he
goes to the field, or pays his portion of the charge, as the
fovereign of his own poffeffions; and when he is conquered a monarch falls.

THE remark, which the Abbe in the conclufion of the
paffage has made, refpecting America contracting debts
in the time of her profperity, (by which he means, before the breaking out of hoftilities) ferves to fhow, though
he has not made the application, the very great commercial difference between a dependent and an independent
country. In a ftate of dependence, and with a fettered commerce, though with all the advantages of peace, her trade
could not balance itfelf, and fhe annually run into debt.
But now, in a ftate of independence, though involved in
war, fhe requires no credit; her ftores are full of mer-
chandize, and gold and filver are become the currency of
the country. How thefe things have eftablifhed themfelves
are difficult to account for: But they are facts, and facts
are more powerful than arguments.

As it is probable this letter will undergo a republica-
tion in Europe, the remarks here thrown together will
ferve to fhow the extreme folly of Britain in refting her
hopes of fuccefs on the extinction of our paper currency.
The expectation is at once fo childifh and forlorn, that
it places her in the laughable condition of a famifhed lion
watching for prey at a fpider's web.

FROM this account of the currency, the Abbe proceeds
to ftate the condition of America in the winter 1777, and
the

the fpring following; and clofes his obfervations with
mentioning the treaty of alliance, which was figned in
France, and the propofitions of the Britifh Miniftry,
which were rejected in America. But in the manner in
which the Abbe has arranged his facts, there is a very
material error, that not only he, but other European
hiftorians have fallen into ; none of them having affigned
the true caufe why the Britifh propofals were rejected,
and all of them have affigned a wrong one.

In the winter 1777, and fpring following, Congrefs
were affembled at York-town in Pennfylvania, the Britifh were in poffeffion of Philadelphia, and General
Wafhington with the army were encamped in huts at the
Valley-Forge, twenty-five miles diftant therefrom. To
all, who can remember, it was a feafon of hardfhip, but
not of defpair ; and the Abbe, fpeaking of this period and
its inconveniences, fays,

" A multitude of privations, added to fo many other
" misfortunes, might make the Americans regret their
" former tranquility, and incline them to an accommo-
" dation with England. In vain had the people been
" bound to the new government by the facrednefs of oaths
" and the influence of religion. In vain had endeavours
" been ufed to convince them that it was impoffible to
" treat fafely with a country, in which one parliament
" might overturn, what fhould have been eftablifhed by
" another. In vain had they been threatened with the
" eternal refentment of an exafperated and vindictive ene-
" my. It was poffible that thefe diftant troubles might
" not be balanced by the weight of prefent evils.

" So

" " So thought the Britifh miniftry, when they fent to
" the New World public agents, authorized to offer eve-
" ry thing except independence to thefe very Americans,
" from whom they had two years before exacted an un-
" conditional fubmiffion. It is not improbable, but that
" by this plan of conciliation, a few months fooner, fome
" effect might have been produced. But at the period,
" at which it was propofed by the Court of London, it
" was rejected with difdain, becaufe this meafure appeared
" but as an argument of fear and weaknefs. The people
" were already re-affured. The Congrefs, the Gene-
" rals, the troops, the bold and fkilful men, in each
" colony had poffeffed themfelves of the authority; every
" thing had recovered its firft fpirit. *This was the effect*
" *of a treaty of friendfhip and commerce between the United*
" *States and the Court of Verfailles, figned the 6th of Fe-*
" *bruary,* 1778.

On this paffage of the Abbe's I cannot help remarking, that, to unite time with circumftance, is a material
nicety in hiftory; the want of which frequently throws
it into endlefs confufion and miftake, occafions a total
feparation between caufes and confequences, and connects
them with others they are not immediately, and fometimes not at all, related to.

The Abbe, in faying that the offers of the Britifh
Miniftry "were rejected with difdain," is *right*, as to
the *fact*, but *wrong* as to the *time*; and this error in the
time, has occafioned him to be miftaken in the caufe.

The figning the treaty of Paris the 6th of February,
1778, could have no effect on the mind or politics of
America,

America until it was *known in America*; and therefore, when the Abbe fays, that the rejection of the Britifh offers was in confequence of the alliance, he muft mean, that it was in confequence of the alliance *being known* in America; which was not the cafe: And by this miftake he not only takes from her the reputation, which her unfhaken fortitude in that trying fituation deferves, but is likewife led very injurioufly to fuppofe, that had fhe *not known* of the treaty, the offers would probably have been accepted; whereas fhe knew nothing of the treaty at the time of the rejection, and confequently did not reject them on that ground.

THE propofitions or offers above mentioned were contained in two bills brought into the Britifh Parliament by Lord North on the 17th of February, 1778. Thofe bills were hurried thro' both Houfes with unufual hafte, and before they had gone thro' all the cuftomary forms of Parliament, copies of them were fent over to Lord Howe and General Howe, then in Philadelphia, who were likewife Commiffioners. General Howe ordered them to be printed in Philadelphia, and fent copies of them by a flag to General Wafhington, to be forwarded to Congrefs at Yorktown, where they arrived the 21ft of April, 1778. Thus much for the arrival of the bills in America.

CONGRESS, as is their ufual mode, appointed a committee from their own body, to examine them and report thereon. The report was brought in the next day (the twenty-fecond) was read, and unanimoufly agreed to, entered on their journals, and publifhed for the information of the country. Now this report muft be the rejection

tion to which the Abbe alludes, becaufe Congrefs gave no other formal opinion on thofe bills and propofitions: And on a fubfequent application from the Britifh Commiffioners, dated the 27th of May, and received at York-Town the 6th of June, Congrefs immediately referred them for an anfwer to their printed refolves of the 22d of April. Thus much for the rejection of the offers.

On the 2d of May, that is, eleven days after the above rejection was made, the treaty between the United States and France arrived at Yorktown; and until this moment Congrefs had not the leaft notice or idea, that fuch a meafure was in any train of execution. But left this declaration of mine fhould pafs only for affertion, I fhall fupport it by proof, for it is material to the character and principle of the revolution to fhow, that no condition of America, fince the declaration of independence, however trying and fevere, ever operated to produce the moft diftant idea of yielding it up either by force, diftrefs, artifice or perfuafion. And this proof is the more neceffary, becaufe it was the fyftem of the Britifh Miniftry at this time, as well as before and fince, to hold out to the European powers that America was unfixt in her refolutions and policy; hoping by this artifice to leffen her reputation in Europe, and weaken the confidence which thofe powers or any of them might be inclined to place in her.

At the time thefe matters were tranfacting, I was fecretary in the foreign department of Congrefs. All the *political* letters from the American Commiffioners refted in my hands, and all that were officially written went from my office; and fo far from Congrefs knowing any thing

of

of the figning the treaty, at the time they rejected the
Britifh offers, they had not received a line of information
from their Commiffioners at Paris on any fubject whatever
for upwards of a twelve month. Probably the lofs of the
port of Philadelphia and the navigation of the Delaware,
together with the danger of the feas, covered at this time
with Britifh cruizers, contributed to the difappointment.

ONE packet, it is true, arrived at York-town in January preceding, which was about three months before
the arrival of the treaty; but, ftrange as it may appear,
every letter had been taken out, before it was put on
board the veffel which brought it from France, and blank
white paper put in their ftead.

HAVING thus ftated the time when the propofals from
the Britifh Commiffioners were firft received, and likewife
the time when the treaty of alliance arrived, and fhewn
that the rejection of the former was eleven days prior to
the arrival of the latter, and without the leaft knowledge
of fuch circumftance having taken place or being about
to take place; the rejection, therefore, muft, and ought
to be attributed to the fixt unvaried fentiments of America refpecting the enemy fhe is at war with, and her determination to fupport her independence to the laft poffible
effort, and not to any new circumftance in her favour,
which at that time fhe did not and could not know of.

BESIDES, there is a vigour of determination and fpirit of
defiance in the language of the rejection, (which I here fub-
join) which derive their greateft glory by appearing before
the treaty was known; for that, which is bravery in diftrefs
becomes infult in profperity : And the treaty placed America

on

on fuch a ftrong foundation, that had fhe then known it, the anfwer which fhe gave, would have appeared rather as an air of triumph, than as the glowing ferenity of fortitude.

Upon the whole, the Abbe appears to have entirely miftaken the matter; for inftead of attributing the rejection of the propofitions to *our knowledge* of the treaty of alliance; he fhould have attributed the origin of them in the Britifh cabinet, to *their knowledge* of that event. And then the reafon why they were hurried over to Amemerica in the ftate of bills, that is, before they were paffed into acts, is eafily accounted for, which is, that they might have the chance of reaching America before any knowledge of the treaty fhould arrive, which they were lucky enough to do, and there met the fate they fo richly merited. That thefe bills were brought into the Britifh Parliament after the treaty with France was figned, is proved from the dates: The treaty being on the 6th, and the bills the 17th of February. And that the figning the treaty was known in Parliament, when the bills were brought in, is likewife proved by a fpeech of Mr. Charles Fox, on the faid 17th of February, who, in reply to Lord North, informed the Houfe of the treaty being figned, and challenged the Minifter's knowledge of the fame fact. *)

E 2   Though

---

*) In CONGRESS, April 22d, 1778.

" THE Committee to whom was referred the General's letter of the 18th, containing a certain printed paper fent from Philadelphia, purporting to be the draught of a Bill for declaring the *intenfions* of the Parliament of Great-Britain, as to the *exercife* of what they are pleafed to term their *right* of impofing taxes within thefe United States; and alfo the draught of a Bill to enable the King of Great-Britain to appoint Com-

THOUGH I am not furprifed to fee the Abbe miftaken in matters of hiftory, acted at fo great a diftance from his fphere

---

miffioners, with powers to treat, confult and agree upon the means of quieting certain diforders within the faid States, beg leave to obferve,

" THAT the faid paper being induftrioufly circulated by emiffaries of the enemy, in a partial and fecret manner, the fame ought to be forthwith printed for the public information.

" THE Committee cannot afcertain whether the contents of the faid paper have been framed in Philadelphia, or in Great-Britain, much lefs whether the fame are really and truly intended to be brought into the Parliament of that kingdom, or whether the faid Parliament will confer thereon the ufual folemnities of their laws. But are inclined to believe this will happen, for the following reafons:

" 1ft. BECAUSE their General hath made divers feeble efforts to fet on foot fome kind of treaty during the laft winter, though, either from a miftaken idea of his own dignity and importance, the want of information, or fome other caufe, he hath not made application to thofe who are invefted with a proper authority.

" 2dly. BECAUSE they fuppofe that the fallacious idea of a ceffation of hoftilities will render thefe States remifs in their preparations for war.

3dly. BECAUSE believing the Americans wearied with war, they fuppofe we will accede to their terms for the fake of peace.

4thly. BECAUSE they fuppofe that our negociations may be fubject to a like corrupt influence with their debates.

" 5thly. BECAUSE they expect from this ftep the fame effects they did from what one of their minifters thought proper to call his *conciliatory motion*, viz. that it will prevent foreign powers from giving aid to thefe States; that it will lead their own fubjects to continue a little longer the prefent war; and that it will detach fome weak men in America from the caufe of freedom and virtue.

" 6thly. BECAUSE their King, from his own fhewing, hath reafon to apprehend that his fleets and armies, inftead of being employed againft the territories of thefe States, will be neceffary for the defence of his own dominions. And

" 7thly. BECAUSE the impracticability of fubjugating this country being every day more and more manifeft, it is their intereft to extricate themfelves from the war upon any terms.

" THE Committee beg leave further to obferve, That, upon a fuppofition the matters contained in the faid paper will really

fphere of immediate obfervation, yet I am more than furprifed to find him wrong, (or at leaft what appears fo to
me)

---

go into the Britifh Statute Book, they ferve to fhew, in a clear
point of view, the weaknefs and wickednefs of the enemy.

" THEIR WEAKNESS,

" ıft. BECAUSE they formerly declared, not only that they
had a right to bind the inhabitants of thefe States in all cafes
whatfoever, but alfo that the faid inhabitants fhould *abfolutely*
and *unconditionally* fubmit to the exercife of that right. And
this fubmiffion they have endeavoured to exact by the fword.
Receding from this claim, therefore, under the prefent circumftances, fhews their inability to enforce it.

" 2dly. BECAUSE their Prince hath heretofore rejected the
humbleft petitions of the Reprefentatives of America, praying
to be confidered as fubjects, and protected in the enjoyment of
peace, liberty and fafety ; and hath waged a moft cruel war
againft them, and employed the favages to butcher innocent
women and children. But now the fame Prince pretends to
treat with thofe very Reprefentatives, and grant to the *arms* of
America what he refufed to her *prayers*.

" 3dly. BECAUSE they have uniformly laboured to conquer
this continent, rejecting every idea of accomodation propofed to
them, from a confidence in their own ftrength. Wherefore it
is evident, from the change in their mode of attack, that they
have loft this confidence. And

" 4thly. BECAUSE the conftant language, fpoken not only
by their Minifters, but by the moft public and authentic acts of
the nation, hath been, that it is incompatible with their dignity to treat with the Americans while they have arms in their
hands. Notwithftanding which, an offer is now about to be
made for treaty.

" THE WICKEDNESS and INSINCERITY of the enemy appear from the following confiderations :

" ıft. EITHER the *Bills* now to be paffed contain a direct or
indirect ceffion of a part of their former claims, or they do not.
If they do, then it is acknowledged that they have facrificed
many brave men in an unjuft quarrel. If they do not, then
they are calculated to deceive America into terms, to which
neither argument before the war, nor force fince, could procure
her affent.

" 2dly. THE firft of thefe *Bills* appears, from the title, to
be a declaration of the *intentions* of the Britifh Parliament con-
cerning the exercife of the *right of impofing taxes* within thefe
States. Wherefore, fhould thefe States treat under the faid

me) in the well enlightened field. of philofophical re-flection. Here the materials are his own; created by him-felf; and the error therefore, is an act of the mind.

HITHERTO

Bill, they would *indirectly* acknowledge that right, to obtain which acknowledgment the prefent war hath been avowedly undertaken and profecuted on the part of Great-Britain.

" 3dly. SHOULD fuch pretended right be fo acquiefced in, then, of confequence, the fame might be exercifed whenever the Britifh Parliament fhould find themfelves in a different *temper* and *difpofition*; fince it muft depend upon thofe, and fuch like contingencies, how far men will act according to their former *intentions.*

4thly. THE faid firft Bill, in the body thereof, containeth no new matter, but is precifely the fame with the motion be-fore-mentioned, and liable to all the objections which lay againft the faid motion, excepting the following particular, viz. that *by the motion* actual taxation was to be fufpended, fo long as America fhould give as much as the faid Parliament might think pro-per: Whereas, *by the propofed Bill*, it is to be fufpended, as long as future Parliaments continue of the fame mind with the prefent.

" 5thly. FROM the fecond Bill it appears, that the Britifh King may, if he pleafes, appoint Commiffioners to *treat* and *agree* with thofe, whom they pleafe, about a variety of things therein mentioned. But fuch treaties and agreements are to be of no validity without the concurrence of the faid Parliament, except fo far as they relate to the *fufpenfion* of hoftilities, and of certain of their acts, the granting of pardons, and the appoint-ing of Governors to thefe fovereign, free and indepentend States. Wherefore, the faid Parliament have referved to them-felves, in *exprefs words*, the power of fetting afide any fuch treaty, and taking the advantage of any circumftances which may arife to fubject this continent to their ufurpations.

" 6thly. THE faid Bill, by holding forth a tender of par-don, implies a criminality in our juftifiable refiftance, and con-fequently, to treat under it would be an implied acknowledg-ment, that the inhabitants of thefe States were, what Britain has declared them to be, *Rebels.*

" 7thly. THE inhabitants of thefe States being claimed by them as fubjects, they may.infer, from the nature of the nego-ciation now pretended to be fet on foot, that the faid inhabitants would of right be afterwards bound by fuch laws as they fhould make. Wherefore any agreement entered into on fuch nego-ciation might at any future time be repealed. And

8thly. BECAUSE the faid Bill purports, that the Commif-

HITHERTO my remarks have been confined to circumstances; the order in which they arofe, and the events they

---

fioners therein mentioned may treat with private individuals; a meafure highly derogatory to the dignity of national character.

"FROM all which it appears evident to your Committee, that the faid Bills are intended to operate upon the hopes and fears of the good people of thefe States, fo as to create divifions among them, and a defection from the common caufe, now by the blefling of Divine Providence drawing near to a favourable iffue. That they are the fequel of that infidious plan, which, from the days of the Stamp-act down to the prefent time, hath involved this country in contention and bloodfhed. And that, as in other cafes fo in this, although circumftances may force them at times to recede from their unjuftifiable claims, there can be no doubt but they will as heretofore, upon the firft favourable occafion, again difplay that luft of domination, which hath rent in twain the mighty empire of Britain.

"UPON the whole matter, the Committee beg leave to report it as their opinion, that as the Americans united in this arduous conteft upon principles of common intereft, for the defence of common rights and privileges, which union hath been cemented by common calamities and by mutual good offices and affection, fo the great caufe for which they contend, and in which all mankind are interefted, muft derive its fuccefs from the continuance of that union. Wherefore any man or body of men, who fhould prefume to make any feparate or partial convention or agreement with Commiffioners under the crown of Great-Britain, or any of them, ought to be confidered and treated as open and avowed enemies of thefe United States.

" And further your Committee beg leave to report it as their opinion, That thefe United States cannot, with propriety, hold any conference or treaty with *any* Commiffioners on the part of Great-Britain, unlefs they fhall, as a preliminary thereto, either withdraw their fleets and armies, or elfe, in pofitive and exprefs terms, acknowledge the Independence of the faid States.

" AND inafmuch as it appears to be the defign of the enemies of thefe States to lull them into a fatal fecurity—to the end that they may act with a becoming weight and importance, it is the opinion of your Committee, that the feveral States be called upon to ufe the moft ftrenuous exertions to have their refpective quotas of continental troops in the field as foon as poffible, and that all the militia of the faid States be held in readinefs, to act as occafion may require.".

they produced. In thefe, my information being better than the Abbe's, my tafk was eafy. How I may fucceed in controverting matters of fentiment and opinion, with one whom years, experience, and long eftablifhed repu- tation have placed in a fuperior line, I am lefs confident in; but as they fall within the fcope of my obfervations it would be improper to pafs them over.

FROM this part of the Abbe's work to the latter end, I find feveral expreffions, which appear to me to ftart, with a cynical complexion, from the path of liberal think- ing, or at leaft they are fo involved as to lofe many of the beauties which diftinguifh other parts of the performance.

THE Abbe having brought his work to the period when

The following is the anfwer of Congrefs to the fecond applica- tion to the Commiffioners :

York-Town, June 6, 1778.

SIR,

I HAVE had the honor of laying your letter of the 3d in- ftant, with the acts of the Britifh Parliament which came inclofed, before Congrefs; and I am inftructed to acquaint you, Sir, that they have already expreffed their fentiments upon bills, not effentially different from thofe acts, in a publication of the 22d of April laft.

"BE affured, Sir, when the King of Great-Britain fhall be ferioufly difpofed to put an end to the unprovoked and cruel war waged againft thefe United States, Congrefs will readily attend to fuch terms of peace, as may confift with the honor of independent nations, the intereft of their conftituents, and the facred regard they mean to pay to treaties. I have the honor to be, Sir,

Your moft obedient, and
moft humble fervant,
HENRY LAURENS,
Prefident of Congrefs."

His Excellency
Sir Henry Clinton, K. B. Philad.

when the treaty of alliance between France and the United States commenced, proceeds to make some remarks thereon.

" In fhort," fays he, " philofophy, whofe firft fenti-
" ment is the defire to fee all governments juft and all
" people happy, in cafting her eyes upon this alliance of
" a monarchy, with a people, who are defending their
" liberty, *is curious to know its motive. She fees, at once,*
" *too clearly, that the happinefs of mankind has no part in it.*"

WHATEVER train of thinking or of temper the Abbe might be in, when he penned this expreffion, matters not. They will neither qualify the fentiment, nor add to its de-fect. If right, it needs no apology; if wrong, it merits no excufe. It is fent into the world as an opinion of philofophy, and may be examined without regard to the author.

IT feems to be a defect, connected with ingenuity, that it often employs itfelf more in matters of curiofity, than ufefulnefs. Man muft be the privy counfellor of fate, or fomething is not right. He muft know the fprings, the whys and wherefores of every thing, or he fits down unfa-tisfied. Whether this be a crime, or only a caprice of hu-manity, I am not enquiring into. I fhall take the paffage as I find it, and place my objections againft it.

IT is not fo properly the *motives* which *produced* the al-liance, as the *confequences* which are to be *produced from it,* that mark out the field of philofophical reflection. In the one we only penetrate into the barren cave of fecrecy, where little can be known, and every thing may be mif-

F   conceived;

conceived ; in the other, the mind is prefented with a wide extended profpeɛt of vagetative good, and fees a thoufand bleffings budding into exiftence.

But the expreffion, even within the compafs of the Abbe's meaning, fets out with an error, becaufe it is made to declare that, which no man has authority to declare. Who can fay that the happinefs of mankind made *no part of the motives* which produced the alliance? To be able to declare this, a man muft be poffeffed of the mind of all the parties concerned, and know that their motives were fomething elfe.

In proportion as the independence of America became contemplated and underftood, the local advantages of it to the immediate aɛtors, and the numerous benefits it pro-mifed to mankind, appeared to be every day encreafing; and we faw not a temporary good for the prefent race on-ly, but a continued good to all pofterity; thefe motives, therefore, added to thofe which preceded them, became the motives on the part of America, which led her to propofe and agree to the treaty of alliance, as the beft effeɛtual method of extending and fecuring happinefs; and there-fore, with refpeɛt to us, the Abbe is wrong.

France, on the other hand, was fituated very differently to America. She was not aɛted upon by neceffity to feek a friend, and therefore her motive in becoming one, has the ftrongeft evidence of being good, and that which is fo, muft have fome happinefs for its objeɛt. With regard to herfelf, fhe faw a train of conveniences worthy her atten-tion. By leffening the power of an enemy, whom, at the fame time, fhe fought neither to deftroy nor diftrefs,

fhe

fhe gained an advantage without doing an evil, and created
to herfelf a new friend by affociating with a country in
misfortune. The fprings of thought that lead to actions
of this kind, however political they may be, are neverthelefs naturally beneficient; for in all caufes, good or
bad, it is neceffary there fhould be a fitnefs in the mind,
to enable it to act in character with the object: Therefore
as a bad caufe cannot be profecuted with a good motive,
fo neither can a good caufe be long fupported by a bad
one, and as no man acts without a motive, therefore in
the prefent inftance, as they cannot be bad, they muft be
admitted to be good. But the Abbe fets out upon fuch
an extended fcale, that he overlooks the degrees by which
it is meafured, and rejects the beginning of good, becaufe
the end comes not at once.

It is true that bad motives may in fome degree be
brought to fupport a good caufe or profecute a good object;
but it never continues long, which is not the cafe with
France; for either the object will reform the mind, or
the mind corrupt the object, or elfe not being able, either
way, to get into unifon, they will feparate in difguft:
And this natural, though unperceived progrefs of affocia-
tion or contention between the mind and the object, is the
fecret caufe of fidelity or defection. Every object a man
purfues, is, for the time, a kind of miftrefs to his mind:
if both are good or bad, the union is natural; but if they
are in reverfe, and neither can feduce nor yet reform the
other, the oppofition grows into diflike and a feparation
follows.

When the caufe of America firft made her appearance
on the ftage of the univerfe, there were many, who, in

the

the ftile of adventurers and fortune hunters, were dangling in her train, and making their court to her with every profeffion of honour and attachment. They were loud in her praife and oftentatious in her fervice. Every place echoed with their ardour or their anger, and they feemed like men in love. But, alas, they were fortune hunters. Their expectations were excited, but their minds were unimpreffed; and finding her not to their purpofe, nor themfelves reformed by her influence, they ceafed their fuit, and in fome inftances deferted and betrayed her.

THERE were others, who at firft beheld her with in-difference, and unacquainted with her character were cau-tious of her company. They treated her as one, who, under the fair name of liberty, might conceal the hideous figure of anarchy, or the gloomy monfter of tyranny. They knew not what fhe was. If fair, fhe was fair in-deed. But ftill fhe was fufpected, and though born among us appeared to be a ftranger.

ACCIDENT with fome, and curiofity with others, brought on a diftant acquaintance. They ventured to look at her. They felt an inclination to fpeak to her. One intimacy led to another, till the fufpicion wore away and a change of fentiment ftole gradually upon the mind; and having no felf intereft to ferve, no paffion of difhonour to gratify, they became enamoured of her innocence, and unaltered by misfortune or uninflamed by fuccefs, fhared with fidelity in the varieties of her fate.

THIS declaration of the Abbe's, refpecting motives, has led me unintendedly into a train of metaphyfical rea-foning; but there was no other avenue by which it could

fo

fo properly be approached. To place prefumption againſt prefumption, aſſertion againſt aſſertion, is a mode of oppofition that has no effect; and therefore the more eligible method was to ſhew, that the declaration does not correfpond with the natural progreſs of the mind and the influence it has upon our conduct.---I ſhall now quit this part and proceed to what I have before ſtated, namely, that it is not ſo properly the motives which produced the alliance, as the confequences to be produced from it, that mark out the field of philofophical reflection.

It is an obfervation I have already made in fome former publication, that the circle of civilization is yet incomplete. A mutuality of wants have formed the individuals of each country into a kind of national fociety, and here the progreſs of civilization has ſtopt. For it is eafy to fee, that nations with regard to each other (notwithſtanding the ideal civil law which every one explains as it ſuits him) are like individuals in a ſtate of nature. They are regulated by no fixt principle, governed by no compulfive law, and each does independently what it pleafes or what it can.

Were it poſſible we could have known the world when in a ſtate of barbariſm, we might have concluded, that it never could be brought into the order we now fee it. The untamed mind waş then as hard, if not harder, to work upon in its individual ſtate, than the national mind is in its prefent one. Yet we have feen the accompliſhment of the one, why then ſhould we doubt that of the other.

There is a greater fitneſs in mankind to extend and
compleat

compleat the civilization of nations with each other at this day, than there was to begin it with the unconnected individuals at firſt; in the ſame manner that it is ſomewhat eaſier to put together the materials of a machine after they are formed, than it was to form them from original matter. The preſent condition of the world differing ſo exceedingly from what it formerly was, has given a new caſt to the mind of man, more than what he appears to be ſenſible of. The want of the individual, which firſt produced the idea of ſociety, are now augmented into the wants of the nation, and he is obliged to ſeek from another country what before he ſought from the next perſon.

LETTERS, the tongue of the world, have in ſome meaſure brought all mankind acquainted, and by an extenſion of their uſes are every day promoting ſome new friendſhip. Through them diſtant nations become capable of converſation, and loſing by degrees the awkwardneſs of ſtrangers, and the moroſeneſs of ſuſpicion, they learn to know and underſtand each other. Science, the partiſan of no country, but the beneficient patroneſs of all, has liberally opened a temple where all may meet. Her influence on the mind, like the ſun on the chilled earth, has long been preparing it for higher cultivation and further improvement. The philoſopher of one country ſees not an enemy in the philoſopher of another : He takes his ſeat in the temple of ſcience and aſks not who ſits beſide him.

THIS was not the condition of the barbarian world. Then the wants of man were few and the objects within his reach. While he could acquire theſe, he lived in a

ſtate

ftate of individual independence, the confequence of which was, there were as many nations as perfons, each contending with the other, to fecure fomething which he had, or to obtain fomething which he had not. The world had then no bufinefs to follow, no ftudies to exercife the mind. Their time was divided between floth and fatigue. Hunting and war were their chief occupations; fleep and food their principal enjoyments.

Now it is otherwife. A change in the mode of life has made it neceffary to be bufy; and man finds a thoufand things to do now which before he did not. Inftead of placing his ideas of greatnefs in the rude atchievements of the favage, he ftudies arts, fcience, agriculture and commerce, the refinements of the gentleman, the principals of fociety and the knowledge of the philofopher.

There are many things which in themfelves are morally neither good nor bad, but they are productive of confequences, which are ftrongly marked with one or other of thefe characters. Thus commerce, though in itfelf a moral nullity, has had a confiderable influence in tempering the human mind. It was the want of objects in the ancient world, which occafioned in them fuch a rude and perpetual turn for war. Their time hung on their hands without the means of employment. The indolence they lived in afforded leafure for mifchief, and being all idle at once, and equal in their circumftances, they were eafily provoked or induced to action.

But the introduction of commerce furnifhed the world with objects, which, in their extent, reach every man and give him fomething to think about and fomething to
do;

do; by thefe his attention is mechanically drawn from the purfuits, which a ftate of indolence and an unemployed mind occafioned, and he trades with the fame countries, which former ages, tempted by their productions, and too indolent to purchafe them, would have gone to war with.

THUS, as I have already obferved, the condition of the world being materially changed by the influence of fcience and commerce, it is put into a fitnefs not only to admit of, but to defire, an extenfion of civilization. The principal and almoft only remaining enemy it now has to encounter, is *prejudice*; for it is evidently the intereft of mankind to agree and make the beft of life. The world has undergone its divifions of empire, the feveral boundaries of which are known and fettled. The idea of conquering countries like the Greeks and Romans does not now exift; and experience has exploded the notion of going to war for the fake of profit. In fhort, the objects for war are exceedingly diminifhed, and there is now left fcarcely any thing to quarrel about, but what arifes from that demon of fociety, prejudice, and the confequent fullennefs and untractablenefs of the temper.

THERE is fomething exceedingly curious in the conftitution and operation of prejudice. It has the fingular ability of accomodating itfelf to all the poffible varieties of the human mind. Some paffions and vices are but thinly fcattered among mankind, and find only here and there a fitnefs of reception. But prejudice like the fpider makes every where its home. It has neither tafte nor choice of place, and all that it requires is room. There is fcarcely a fituation, except fire or water, in which a fpider will not live. So let the mind be as naked, as the walls of an empty
and

and forfaken tenement, gloomy as a dungeon, or orna-
mented with the richeft abilities of thinking, let it be hot,
cold, dark or light, lonely or inhabited, ftill prejudice,
if undifturbed, will fill it with cobwebs, and live, like
the fpider, where there feems nothing to live on. If the
one prepares her food by poifoning it to her palate and
her ufe, the other does the fame; and as feveral of our
paffions are ftrongly charactered by the animal world, prejudice may be denominated the fpider of the mind.

PERHAPS no two events ever united fo intimately and
forceably to combat and expel prejudice, as the Revolution of America and the Alliance with France. Their
effects are felt, and their influence already extends as well
to the old world as the new. Our ftile and manner of
thinking have undergone a revolution, more extraordinary
than the political revolution of the country. We fee with
other eyes; we hear with other ears; and think with other
thoughts, than thofe we formerly ufed. We can look
back on our own prejudices, as if they had been the prejudices of other people. We now fee and know they
were prejudices and nothing elfe, and relieved from their
fhackles enjoy a freedom of mind, we felt not before. It
was not all the argument, however powerful, nor all the
reafoning, however elegant, that could have produced
this change, fo neceffary to the extenfion of the mind,
and the cordiality of the world, without the two circumftances of the Revolution and the Alliance.

HAD America dropt quietly from Britain, no material
change, in fentiment, had taken place. The fame notions,
prejudices, and conceits, would have governed in both
countries, as governed them before, and ftill the flaves of

G   error

error and education, they would have travelled on in the beaten track of vulgar and habitual thinking. But brought about by the means it has been, both with regard to ourselves, to France, and to England, every corner of the mind is fwept of its cobwebs, poifon, and duft, and made fit for the reception of generous happinefs.

PERHAPS there never was an Alliance on a broader bafis, than that between America and France, and the progrefs of it is worth attending to. The countries had been enemies, not properly of themfelves, but through the medium of England. They, originally, had no quarrel with each other, nor any caufe for one, but what arofe from the intereft of England and her arming America againft France. At the fame time, the Americans at a diftance from, and unacquainted with the world, and tutored in all the prejudices which governed thofe who governed them, conceived it their duty to act as they were taught. In doing this, they expended their fubftance to make conquefts, not for themfelves but for their mafters, who in return treated them as flaves.

A long fucceffion of infolent feverity, and the feparation finally occafioned by the commencement of hoftilities at Lexington, on the 19th of April, 1775, naturally produced a new difpofition of thinking. As the mind clofed itfelf towards England, it opened itfelf towards the world, and our prejudices like our oppreffions underwent, though lefs obferved, a mental examination; until we found the former as inconfiftent with reafon and benevolence, as the latter were repugnant to our civil and political rights.

WHILE we were thus advancing by degrees into the wide field of extended humanity, the alliance with France

was

was concluded. An alliance not formed for the meer purpofe of a day, but on juft and generous grounds, and with equal and mutual advantages; and the eafy affectionate manner in which the parties have fince communicated, has made it an alliance-not of courts only but of countries. There is now an union of mind as well as of intereft; and our hearts as well as our profperity call on us to fupport it.

THE people of England not having experienced this change, had likewife no idea of it. They were hugging to their bofoms the fame prejudices we were trampling beneath our feet; and they expected to keep a hold upon America, by that narrownefs of thinking, which America difdained. What they were proud of, we difpifed; and this is a principal caufe why all their negociations, conftructed on this ground, have failed. We are now really another people, and cannot again go back to ignorance and prejudice. The mind once enlightened cannot again become dark. There is no poffibility, neither is there any term to exprefs the fuppofition by, of the mind, unknowing any thing it already knows; and therefore all attempts on the part of England, fitted to the former habit of America, and on the expectation of their applying now, will be like perfuading a feeing man to become blind, and a fenfible one to turn an idiot. The firft of which is unnatural, and the other impoffible.

As to the remark which the Abbe makes of the one country being a monarchy and the other a republic, it can have no effential meaning. Forms of government have nothing to do with treaties. The former are the in-

ternal

ternal police of the countries feverally ; the latter, their
external police jointly : and fo long as each performs its
part, we have no more right or bufinefs to know how the
one or the other conducts its domeftic affairs, than we
have to inquire into the private concerns of a family.

BUT had the Abbe reflected for a moment, he would
have feen, that courts or the governing powers of all
countries, be their forms what they may, are relatively
republics with each other. It is the firft and true principle of alliancing. Antiquity may have given precedence,
and power will naturally create importance, but their equal
right is never difputed. It may likewife be worthy of remarking, that a monarchical country can fuffer nothing in
its popular happinefs by allying with a republican one ;
and republican governments have never been deftroyed by
their external connections, but by fome internal convul-
fion or contrivance. France has been in alliance with the
republic of Swifferland for more than two hundred years,
and ftill Swifferland retains her original form as entire as
if fhe had allied with a republic like herfelf ; therefore
this remark of the Abbe goes to nothing.----Befides, it is
beft that mankind fhould mix. There is ever fomething
to learn, either of manners or principle ; and it is by a
free communication, without regard to domeftic matters,
that friendfhip is to be extended, and prejudice deftroyed
all over the world.

BUT notwithftanding the Abbe's high profeffions in
favor of liberty, he appears fometimes to forget himfelf,
or that his theory is rather the child of his fancy than of
his judgement : For in almoft the fame inftant that he

cenfures

cenfures the alliance as not originally or fufficiently calculated for the happinefs of mankind, he, by a figure of
implication, accufes France for having acted fo generoufly and unrefervedly in concluding it. "Why did they,
" (fays he, meaning the Court of France) tie themfelves
" down by an inconfiderate treaty to conditions with the
" Congrefs, which they might themfelves have held in
" dependence by ample and regular fupplies."

When an author untertakes to treat of public happinefs, he ought to be certain that he does not miftake paffion for right, nor imagination for principle. Principle,
like truth, needs no contrivance. It will ever tell its
own tale, and tell it the fame way. But where this is not
the cafe, every page muft be watched, recollected, and
compared, like an invented ftory.

I am furprifed at this paffage of the Abbe. It means
nothing or it means ill ; and in any cafe it fhews the
great difference between fpeculative and practical knowledge. A treaty according to the Abbe's language would
have neither duration nor affection ; it might have
lafted to the end of the war, and then expired with it.---
But France, by acting in a ftile fuperior to the little politics of narrow thinking, has eftablifhed a generous fame
and won the love of a country fhe was before a ftranger
to. She had to treat with a people who thought as nature
taught them ; and, on her own part, fhe wifely faw,
there was no prefent advantage to be obtained by unequal
terms, which could balance the more lafting ones that
might flow from a kind and generous beginning.

From this part the Abbe advances into the fecret tranf-
actions of the two Cabinets of Verfailles and Madrid refpecting

fpecting the independence of America; through which
I mean not to follow him. It is a circumftance fufficiently ftriking without being commented on, that the former union of America with Britain produced a power,
which in her hands, was becoming dangerous to the world:
And there is no improbability in fuppofing, that had the
latter known as much of the ftrength of the former, before fhe began the quarrel as fhe has known fince, that
inftead of attempting to reduce her to unconditional fubmiffion, fhe would have propofed to her the conqueft of
Mexico. But from the countries feparately Spain has
nothing to apprehend, though from their union fhe had
more to fear than any other power in Europe.

THE part which I fhall more particularly confine myfelf to, is that wherein the Abbe takes an opportunity of
complimenting the Britifh Miniftry with high encomiums
of admiration, on their rejecting the offered mediation of
the court of Madrid, in 1779.

IT muft be remembered that before Spain joined France
in the war, fhe undertook the office of a mediator and
made propofals to the Britifh King and Miniftry fo exceedingly favorable to their intereft, that had they been
accepted, would have become inconvenient, if not inad-
miffible, to America. Thefe propofals were neverthelefs
rejected by the Britifh cabinet; on which the Abbe fays,--

" It is in fuch a circumftance as this ; it is in the time
" when noble pride elevates the foul fuperior to all terror;
" when nothing is feen more dreadful than the fhame of
" receiving the law, and when there is no doubt or hefi-
" tation which to chufe, between ruin and difhonour ;
" it

" it is then, that the greatnefs of a nation is difplayed.
" I acknowledge however that men, accuftomed to judge
" of things by the event, call great and perilous refolu-
" tions, heroifm or madnefs, according to the good or
" bad fuccefs with which they have been attended. If
" then, I fhould be afked, what is the name which fhall
" in years to come be given to the firmnefs, which was
" in this moment exhibited by the Englifh, I fhall anfwer
" that I do not know. But that which it deferves I know.
" I know that the annals of the world hold out to us but
" rarely, the auguft and majeftic fpectacle of a nation,
" which chufes rather to renounce its duration than its
" glory."

In this paragraph the conception is lofty and the expreffion elegant; but the colouring is too high for the
original, and the likenefs fails through an excefs of graces.
To fit the powers of thinking and the turn of language
to the fubject, fo as to bring out a clear conclufion that
fhall hit the point in queftion and nothing elfe, is the true
criterion of writing. But the greater part of the Abbe's
writings (if he will pardon me the remark) appear to me
uncentral and burthened with variety. They reprefent a
beautiful wildernefs without paths; in which the eye is
diverted by every thing, without being particularly directed
to any thing; and in which it is agreeable to be loft, and
difficult to find the way out.

Before I offer any other remark on the fpirit and
compofition of the above paffage, I fhall compare it with
the circumftance it alludes to.

The circumftance then does not deferve the encomium. The rejection was not prompted by her fortitude
but

but her vanity. She did not view it as a case of despair or even of extreme danger, and consequently the determination to renounce her duration rather than her glory, cannot apply to the condition of her mind. She had then high expectations of subjugating America, and had no other naval force against her than France; neither was she certain that rejecting the mediation of Spain would combine that power with France. New mediations might arise more favorable than those she had refused. But if they should not, and Spain should join, she still saw that it would only bring out her naval force against France and Spain, which was not wanted and could not be employed against America, and habits of thinking had taught her to believe herself superior to both.

But in any case to which the consequence might point, there was nothing to impress her with the idea of renouncing her duration. It is not the policy of Europe to suffer the extinction of any power, but only to lop off or prevent its dangerous encrease. She was likewise freed by situation from the internal and immediate horrors of invasion; was rolling in dissipation and looking for conquests; and tho' she suffered nothing but the expence of war, she still had a greedy eye to magnificient reimbursement.

But if the Abbe is delighted with high and striking singularities of character, he might, in America, have found ample field for encomium. Here was a people, who could not know what part the world would take for, or against them; and who were venturing on an untried scheme, in opposition to a power, against which more formidable nations had failed. They had every thing to learn but the principles which supported them, and every

thing

thing to procure that was neceffary for their defence. They have at times feen themfelves as low as diftrefs could make them, without fhowing the leaft .ftagger in their fortitude ; and been raifed again by the moft unexpected. events, without difcovering an unmanly difcompofure of joy. To hefitate or to defpair are conditions equally un-known in America. Her mind was prepared for every thing ; becaufe her original and final refolution of fucceed-ing or perifhing included all poffible circumftances.

THE rejection of the Britifh propofitions in the year 1778, circumftanced as America was at that time, is a far greater inftance of unfhaken fortitude than the refufal of the Spanifh mediation by the Court of London : And other hiftorians, befides the Abbe, ftruck with the vaftnefs of her conduct therein, have, like himfelf, attributed it to a circumftance, which was then unknown, the alliance with France. Their error fhews their idea of its great-nefs ; becaufe, in order to account for it, they have fought a caufe fuited to its magnitude, without knowing that the caufe exifted in the principles of the country. *)

---

*) Extract from " *A fhort review of the prefent reign*" in England.

Page 45. in the New Annual Regifter for the year 1780.

" THE *Commiffioners, who, in confequence of Lord North's*
" *conciliatory bills, went over to America, to propofe terms*
" *of peace to the colonies, were wholly unfuccefsful. The con-*
" *ceffions which formerly would have been received with the*
" *utmoft gratitude,* ' *were rejected with difdain.* Now was
" *the time of American pride and haughtinefs. It is probable,*
" *however, that it was not pride and haughtinefs alone that*
" *dictated the Refolutions of Congrefs, but a diftruft of the*
" *fincerity of the offers of Britain, a determination not to give*
" *up their independence, and,* ABOVE ALL, THE ENGAGE-
" MENTS INTO WHICH THEY HAD ENTERED BY
" THEIR LATE TREATY WITH FRANCE." .

H   BUT

But this paffionate encomium of the Abbe is deferved-
ly fubject to moral and philofophical objections. It is the
effufion of wild thinking, and has a tendency to prevent
that humanity of reflection which the criminal conduct of
Britain enjoins on her as a duty.---It is a laudanum to
courtly iniquity.----It keeps in intoxicated fleep the con-
fcience of a nation ; and more mifchief is effected by
wrapping up guilt in fplendid excufe, than by directly
patronizing it.

Britain is now the only country which holds the
world in difturbance and war ; and inftead of paying com-
pliments to the excefs of her crimes, the Abbe would have
appeared much more in character, had he put to her, or
to her monarch, this ferious queftion---

Are there not miferies enough in the world, too difficult to be encountered and too pointed to be borne, without ftudying to enlarge the lift and arming it with new
deftruction ? Is life fo very long, that it is neceffary, nay
even a duty, to fhake the fand and haften out the period
of duration ? Is the path fo elegantly fmooth, fo decked
on every fide and carpeted with joys, that wretchednefs is
wanted to enrich it as a foil ? Go afk thine aching heart
when forrow from a thoufand caufes wound it, go afk thy
fickened felf when every medicine fails, whether this
be the cafe or not ?

Quitting my remarks on this head, I proceed to
another, in which the Abbe has let loofe a vein of ill
nature, and, what is ftill worfe, of injuftice.

After cavilling at the treaty, he goes on to characterize
the

the feveral parties combined in the war---" Is it poffible," fays the Abbe, " that a ftrict union fhould long fubfift " amongft confederates of characters fo oppofite as the " hafty, light, diftainful Frenchman, the jealous, haugh- " ty, fly, flow, circumfpective Spaniard, and the Ame- " rican, who is fecretly fnatching looks at the mother " country, and would rejoice, were they compatible with " his independence, at the difafters of his allies."

To draw foolifh portraits of each other, is a mode of attack and reprifal, which the greater part of mankind are fond of indulging. The ferious philofopher fhould be above it, more efpecially in cafes from which no poffible good can arife, and mifchief may, and where no received provocation can palliate the offence.---The Abbe might have invented a difference of character for every country in the world, and they in return might find others for him, till in the war of wit all real character is loft. The plea- fantry of one nation or the gravity of another may, by a little penciling, be diftorted into whimfical features, and the painter become as much laughed at as the painting.

But why did not the Abbe look a little deeper and bring forth the excellencies of the feveral parties. Why did he not dwell with pleafure on that greatnefs of cha- racter, that fuperiority of heart, which has marked the conduct of France in her conquefts, and which has forced an acknowledgment even from Britain.

There is one line, at leaft, (and many others might be difcovered) in which the confederates unite, which is, that of a rival eminence in their treatment of their ene- mies. Spain, in her conqueft of Minorca and the Bahama

iflands

iſlands confirms this remark. America has been invariable in her lenity from the beginning of the war, notwithſtanding the high provocations ſhe has experienced. It is England only who has been inſolent and cruel.

But why muſt America be charged with a crime undeſerved by her conduct, more ſo by her principles, and which, if a fact, would be fatal to her honor. I mean that of want of attachment to her allies, or rejoicing in their diſaſters. She, it is true, has been aſſiduous in ſhewing to the world that ſhe was not the aggreſſor towards England, that the quarrel was not of her ſeeking, or, at that time, even of her wiſhing. But to draw inferences from her candour, and even from her juſtification, to ſtab her character by, and I ſee nothing elſe from which they can be ſuppoſed to be drawn, is unkind and unjuſt.

Does her rejection of the Britiſh propoſitions in 1779, before ſhe knew of any alliance with France, correſpond with the Abbe's deſcription of her mind? does a ſingle inſtance of her conduct ſince that time juſtify it?---But there is a ſtill better evidence to apply to, which is, that of all the mails, which at different times have been way laid on the road, in divers parts of America, and taken and carried into New-York, and from which the moſt ſecret and confidential private letters, as well as thoſe from authority, have been publiſhed, not one of them, I repeat it, not a ſingle one of them, gives countenance to ſuch a charge.

This is not a country where men are under government reſtraint in ſpeaking; and if there is any kind of

reſtraint

reſtraint, it ariſes from a fear of popular reſentment. Now, if nothing in her private or public correſpondence favours ſuch a ſuggeſtion, and if the general diſpoſition of the country is ſuch as to make it unſafe for a man to ſhew an appearance of joy at any diſaſter to her ally, on what grounds, I aſk, can the accuſation ſtand. What company the Abbe may have kept in France, we cannot know; but this we know, that the account he gives does not apply to America.

HAD the Abbe been in America at the time the news arrived of the diſaſter of the fleet under Count de Graſſe, in the Weſt-Indies, he would have ſeen his vaſt miſtake. Neither do I remember any inſtance, except the loſs of Charleſtown, in which the public mind ſuffered more ſevere and pungent concern, or underwent more agitations of hope and apprehenſion as to the truth or falſhood of the report. Had the loſs been all our own it could not have had a deeper effect, yet it was not one of theſe caſes which reached to the independence of America.

IN the geographical account which the Abbe gives of the Thirteen States, he is ſo exceedingly erroneous, that to attempt a particular refutation, would exceed the limits I have preſcribed to myſelf. And as it is a matter neither political, hiſtorical, nor ſentimental, and which can always be contradicted by the extent and natural circumſtances of the country, I ſhall paſs it over; with this additional remark, that I never yet ſaw an European deſcription of America that was true, neither can any perſon gain a juſt idea of it, but by coming to it.

THOUGH I have already extended this letter beyond
what

what I at firſt propoſed, I am, neverthelefs, obliged to omit many obſervations, I originally defigned to have made. I wiſh there had been no occaſion for making any. But the wrong ideas which the Abbe's work had a tendency to excite, and the prejudicial impreſſions they might make, muſt be an apology for my remarks, and the freedom with which they are done.

I obferve the Abbe has made a ſort of epitome of a confiderable part of the pamphlet *Common Senſe*, and introduced it in that form into his publication. But there are other places where the Abbe has borrowed freely from the ſame pamphlet without acknowledging it. The difference between ſociety and government, with which the pamphlet opens, is taken from it, and in ſome expreſſions almoſt literally, into the Abbe's work as if originally his own; and through the whole of the Abbe's remarks on this head, the idea in Common Senfe is ſo cloſely copied and purſued, that the difference is only in words, and in the arrangement of the thoughts, and not in the thoughts themſelves. *

BUT

---

* COMMON SENSE.

" Some writers have ſo confounded ſociety with government, as to leave little or no diſtinction between them; whereas, they are not only different, but have different origins."

"Society is produced by our wants and governments by our wickedneſs; the former promotes our happineſs *poſitively*, by uniting our affections, the latter *negatively*, by reſtraining our vices."

ABBE RAYNAL.

" Care muſt be taken not to confound together ſociety with government. That they may be known diſtinctly, their origin ſhould be confidered"

" Society originates in the wants of men, government in their vices. Society tends always to good; government ought always to tend to the repreſſing of evil."

BUT as it is time I fhould come to a conclufion of my letter, I fhall forbear all further obfervations on the Abbe's work,

---

In the following paragraphs there is lefs likenefs in the language, but the ideas in the one are evidently copied from the other.

COMMON SENSE.

" In order to gain a clear and juft idea of the defign and end of government, let us fuppofe a fmall number of perfons, meeting in fome fequeftered part of the earth unconnected with the reft; they will then reprefent the peopling of any country or of the world. In this ftate of natural liberty, fociety will be our firft thought. A thoufand motives will excite them thereto. The ftrength of one man is fo unequal to his wants, and his mind fo unfitted for perpetual folitude, that he is foon obliged to feek affiftance of another, who, in his turn, requires the fame. Four or five united would be able to raife a tolerable dwelling in the midft of a wildernefs; but *one* man might labour out the common period of life, without accomplifhing any thing; when he had felled his timber, he could not remove it, nor erect it after it was removed; hunger, in the mean time would urge him from his work, and every different want call him a different way. Difeafe, nay even misfortune, would be death; for though neither might be immediately mortal, yet either of them would difable him

ABBE RAYNAL.

" Man, thrown, as it were, by chance upon the globe, furrounded by all the evils of nature, obliged continually to defend and protect his life againft the ftorms and tempefts of the air, againft the inundations of water, againft the fire of vulcanoes, againft the intemperance of frigid and torrid zones, againft the fterrility of the earth which refufes him ailment, or its baneful fecundity, which makes poifon fpring up beneath his feet; in fhort, againft the claws and teeth of favage beafts, who difpute with him his habitation and his prey, and, attacking his perfon, feem refolved to render themfelves rulers of this globe, of which he thinks himfelf to be the mafter: Man, in this ftate, alone and abandoned to himfelf, could do nothing for his prefervation. It was neceffary, therefore, that he fhould unite himfelf, and affociate with his like, in order to bring together their ftrength and intelligence in common ftock. It is by this union that he has triumphed over fo many evils, that he has fafhioned this globe to his ufe, reftrained the rivers, fubjugated the feas, infured his work, and take a concife view of the ftate of public affairs, fince the time in which that performance was publifhed.

A mind habited to actions of meannefs and injuftice, commits them without reflection, or with a very partial one; for on what other ground than this, can we account for the declaration of war againft the Dutch. To gain an idea of the politics which actuated the Britifh Miniftry to this meafure, we muft enter into the opinion which they, and the Englifh in general, had formed of the temper of the Dutch nation; and from thence infer what their expectation of the confequences would be.

COULD

COMMON SENSE.

from living, and reduce him to a ftate in which he might rather be faid to perifh than to die.—Thus neceffity, like a gravitating power, would form our newly arrived emigrants into fociety, the reciprocal bleffings of which, would fupercede and render the obligations of law and government unneceffary, while they remained perfectly juft to each other. But as nothing but heaven is impregnable to vice, it will unavoidably happen, that in proportion as they furmount the firft difficulties of emigration, which bound them together in a common caufe, they will begin to relax in their duty and attachment to each other, and this remiffnefs will point out the neceffity of eftablifhing fome form of government to fupply the defect of moral virtue."

ABBE RAYNAL.

fubfiftence, conquered a part of the animals in obliging them to ferve him, and driven others far from his empire, to the depth of deferts or of woods, where their number diminifhes from age to age. What a man alone would not have been able to effect, men have executed in concert; and altogether they preferve their work. Such is the origin, fuch the advantages, and the end of fociety.—Government owes its birth to the neceffity of preventing and repreffing the injuries which the affociated individuals had to fear from one another. It is the centinel who watches, in order that the common labours be not difturbed."

COULD they have imagined that Holland would have ſeriouſly made a common cauſe with France, Spain, and America, the Britiſh Miniſtry would never have dared to provoke them. It would have been a madneſs in politics to have done ſo; unleſs their views were to haſten on a period of ſuch emphatic diſtreſs, as ſhould juſtify the conceſſions which they ſaw they muſt one day or other make to the world, and for which they wanted an apology to themſelves.----There is a temper in ſome men which ſeeks a pretence for ſubmiſſion. Like a ſhip diſabled in action, and unfited to continue it, it waits the approach of a ſtill larger one to ſtrike to, and feels relief at the opportunity. Whether this is greatneſs or littleneſs of mind, I am not enquiring into. I ſhould ſuppoſe it to be the latter, becauſe it proceeds from the want of knowing how to bear misfortune in its original ſtate.

BUT the ſubſequent conduct of the Britiſh cabinet has ſhewn that this was not their plan of politics, and conſequently their motives muſt be ſought for in another line.

THE truth is, that the Britiſh had formed a very humble opinion of the Dutch nation. They looked on them as a people who would ſubmit to any thing; that they might inſult them as they liked, plunder them as they pleaſed, and ſtill the Dutch dared not to be provoked.

IF this be taken as the opinion of the Britiſh cabinet, the meaſure is eaſily accounted for; becauſe it goes on the ſuppoſition, that when, by a declaration of hoſtilities, they had robbed the Dutch of ſome millions ſterling, (and to rob them was popular) they could make peace with them again whenever they pleaſed, and on almoſt any terms the Britiſh Miniſtry ſhould propoſe. And no ſooner

I   was

was the plundering committed, than the accomodation was set on foot, and failed.

WHEN once the mind loses the sense of its own dignity, it loses, likewise, the ability of judging of it in another. And the American war has thrown Britain into such a variety of absurd situations, that, arguing from herself, she sees not in what conduct national dignity consists in other countries. From Holland she expected duplicity and submission, and this mistake arose from her having acted, in a number of instances during the present war, the same character herself.

To be allied to, or connected with Britain, seems to be an unsafe and impolitic situation. Holland and America are instances of the reality of this remark. Make those countries the allies of France or Spain, and Britain will court them with civility, and treat them with respect; make them her own allies, and she will insult and plunder them. In the first case, she feels some apprehensions at offending them, because they have support at hand; in the latter, those apprehensions do not exist. Such, however, has hitherto been her conduct.

ANOTHER measure which has taken place since the publication of the Abbe's work, and likewise since the time of my beginning this letter, is the change in the British ministry. What line the new cabinet will pursue respecting America, is at this time unknown; neither is it very material, unless they are seriously disposed to a general and honorable peace.

REPEATED experience has shewn, not only the impracticability of conquering America, but the still higher impossibility of conquering her mind, or recalling her back

to

to her former condition of thinking. Since the commencement of the war, which is now approaching to eight years, thoufands and tens of thoufands have advanced, and are daily advancing into the firft ftage of manhood, who, know nothing of Britain but as a barbarous enemy, and to whom the independence of America appears as much the natural and eftablifhed government of the country, as that of England does to an Englifhman. And on the other hand, thoufands of the aged, who had Britifh ideas, have dropped, and are daily dropping, from the ftage of bufinefs and life. The natural progrefs of generation and decay operates every hour to the difadvantage of Britain. Time and death, hard enemies to contend with, fight conftantly againft her intereft ; and the bills of mortality, in every part of America, are the thermometers of her decline. The children in the ftreets are from their cradle bred to confider her as their only foe. They hear of her cruelties ; of their fathers, uncles, and kindred killed ; they fee the remains of burnt and deftroyed houfes, and the common tradition of the fchool they go to, tells them, *thofe things were done by the Britifh.*

THESE are circumftances which the mere Englifh ftate politician, who confiders man only in a ftate of manhood, does not attend to. He gets entangled with parties coeval or equal with himfelf at home, and thinks not how faft the rifing generation in America is growing beyond his knowledge of them, or they of him. In a few years all perfonal remembrance will be loft, and who is King or Minifter in England, will be little known and fcarcely enquired after.

THE new Britifh adminiftration is compofed of perfons who have ever been againft the war, and who have conftantly reprobated all the violent meafures of the former

one.

one. They confidered the American war as deftructive to themfelves, and oppofed it on that ground. But what are thefe things to America? She has nothing to do with Englifh parties. The ins and the outs are nothing to her. It is the whole country fhe is at war with, or muft be at peace with.

WERE every Minifter in England a *Chatham*, it would now weigh little or nothing in the fcale of American politics. Death has preferved to the memory of this ftatefman, *that fame*, which he, by living, would have loft. His plans and opinions, towards the latter part of his life, would have been attended with as many evil confequences, and as much reprobated here, as thofe of Lord North; and, confidering him a wife man, they abound with inconfiftences amounting to abfurdities.

IT has apparently been the fault of many in the late minority, to fuppofe, that America would agree to certain terms with them, were they in place, which fhe would not ever liften to from the then Adminiftration. This idea can anfwer no other purpofe than to prolong the war; and Britain may, at the expence of many more millions, learn the fatality of fuch miftakes. If the new miniftry wifely avoid this hopelefs policy, they will prove themfelves better pilots, and wifer men, than they are conceived to be; for it is every day expected to fee their bark ftrike upon fome hidden rock and go to pieces.

BUT there is a line in which they may be great. A more brilliant opening needs not to prefent itfelf; and it is fuch a one, as true magnanimity would improve, and humanity rejoice in.

A total reformation is wanted in England. She wants
an expanded mind,---an heart which embraces the univerfe.
Inftead of fhutting herfelf up in an ifland, and quarrelling
with the world, fhe would derive more lafting happinefs,
and acquire more real riches, by generoufly mixing with
it, and bravely faying, I am the enemy of none. It is
not now a time for little contrivances or artful politics.
The European world is too experienced to be impofed
upon, and America too wife to be duped. It muft be
fomething new and mafterly that muft fucceed. The idea
of feducing America from her independence, or corrupting
her from her alliance, is a thought too little for a great
mind, and impoffible for any honeft one, to attempt.
Whenever politics are applied to debauch mankind from
their integrity, and diffolve the virtues of human nature,
they become deteftable; and to be a ftatefman upon this
plan, is to be a commiffioned villain. He who aims at it,
leaves a vacancy in his character, which may be filled up
with the worft of epithets.

If the difpofition of England fhould be fuch, as not to
agree to a general and honorable peace, and that the war
muft, at all events, continue longer, I cannot help
wifhing, that the alliances which America has or may enter into, may become the only objects of the war. She
wants an opportunity of fhewing to the world, that fhe
holds her honor as dear and facred as her independence,
and that fhe will in no fituation forfake thofe, whom
no negociations could induce to forfake her. Peace to
every reflective mind, is a defirable object; but *that peace*
which is accompanied with a ruined character, becomes a
crime to the feducer, and a curfe upon the feduced.

But where is the impoffibility or even the great difficul-

ty

ty of England forming a friendſhip with France and Spain, and making it a national virtue to renounce for ever thoſe prejudiced inveteracies it has been her cuſtom to cheriſh; and which, while they ſerve to ſink her with an encreaſing enormity of debt, by involving her in fruitleſs wars, become likewiſe the bane of her repoſe, and the deſtruction of her manners. We had once the fetters that ſhe has now, but experience has ſhewn us the miſtake, and thinking juſtly has ſet us right.

THE true idea of a great nation is that which extends and promotes the principles of univerſal ſociety. Whoſe mind riſes above the atmoſpheres of local thoughts, and conſiders mankind, of whatever nation or profeſſion they may be, as the work of one Creator. The rage for conqueſt has had its faſhion, and its day. Why may not the amiable virtues have the ſame? The Alexanders and Cæſars of antiquity have left behind them their monuments of deſtruction, and are remembered with hatred; while theſe more exalted characters, who firſt taught ſociety and ſcience, are bleſt with the gratitude of every age and country. Of more uſe was *one* philoſopher, though a heathen, to the world, than all the heathen conquerors that ever exiſted.

SHOULD the preſent revolution be deſtinguiſhed by opening a new ſyſtem of extended civilization, it will receive from heaven the higheſt evidence of approbation; and as this is a ſubject to which the Abbe's powers are ſo eminently ſuited, I recommend it to his attention, with the affection of a friend, and the ardour of a univerſal citizen,

POSTSCRIPT.

SINCE clofing the foregoing letter, fome intima-
tions, refpecting a general peace, have made their
way to America. On what authority or foundation
they ftand, or how near or remote fuch an event may be,
are circumftances I am not inquiring into. But as the
fubject muft fooner or later become a matter of ferious
attention, it may not be improper, even at this early period, candidly to inveftigate fome points that are connected
with it, or lead towards it.

THE independence of America is at this moment as
firmly eftablifhed as that of any other country in a ftate
of war. It is not length of time, but power that gives
ftability. Nations at war know nothing of each other on
the fcore of antiquity. It is their prefent and immediate
ftrength, together with their connections, that muft fupport them. To which we may add, that a right which
originated to-day, is as much a right, as if it had the
fanction of a thoufand years; and therefore the independence and prefent governments of America are in no more
danger of being fubverted, becaufe they are modern, than
that of England is fecure, becaufe it is ancient.

THE politics of Britain, fo far as they refpected America, were originally conceived in idiotifm, and acted in
madnefs. There is not a ftep which bears the fmalleft
trace of rationality. In her management of the war, fhe
has laboured to be wretched, and ftudied to be hated; and
in all her former propofitions for accomodation, fhe has
difcovered a total ignorance of mankind, and of thofe natural and unalterable fenfations by which they are fo ge-
nerally governed. How fhe may conduct herfelf in the
prefent or future bufinefs of negociating a peace, is yet to
be proved.

He is a weak politician who does not underftand human
nature, and penetrate into the effect which meafures of
government will have upon the mind. All the mifcar-
riages of Britain have arifen from this defect. The former
Miniftry acted as if they fuppofed mankind to be *without
a mind*; and the prefent Miniftry, as if America was *without a memory*. The one muft have fuppofed we were in-
capable of feeling; and the other, that we could not remember injuries.

K

THERE

THERE is likewise another line in which politicians miſtake, which is that of not rightly calculating, or rather of misjudging, the conſequence which any given circumſtance will produce. Nothing is more frequent, as well in common as in political life, than to hear people complain, that ſuch or ſuch means produced an event directly contrary to their intentions. But the fault lies in their not judging rightly, what the event would be; for the means produced only its proper and natural conſequence.

IT is very probable, that in a treaty for peace, Britain will contend for ſome poſt or other in North-America; perhaps Canada or Halifax, or both: And I infer this from the known deficiency of her politics, which have ever yet made uſe of means, whoſe natural event was againſt both her intereſt and her expectation. But the queſtion with her ought to be, whether it is worth her while to hold them, and what will be the conſequence.

RESPECTING Canada, one or other of the two following will take place, viz. If Canada ſhould people, it will revolt; and if it do not people, it will not be worth the expence of holding. And the ſame may be ſaid of Halifax, and the country round it. But Canada *never will* people; neither is there any occaſion for contrivances on one ſide or the other, for nature alone will do the whole.

BRITAIN may put herſelf to great expences in ſending ſettlers to Canada; but the deſcendants of thoſe ſettlers will be Americans, as other deſcendants have been before them. They will look round and ſee the neighbouring States ſovereign and free, reſpected abroad and trading at large with the world; and the natural love of liberty, the advantages of commerce, the bleſſings of independence and of a happier climate, and a richer ſoil, will draw them ſouthward, and the effect will be that Britain will ſuſtain the expence, and America reap the advantage.

ONE would think that the experience which Britain has had of America, would entirely ſicken her of all thoughts of continental colonization; and any part which ſhe might retain, will only become to her a field of jealouſy and thorns, of debate and contention, for ever ſtruggling for privileges, and meditating revolt. She may form new ſettlements, but they will be for us; they will become part of the United States of America; and that againſt all her contrivances to prevent it, or without any endeavours of ours to promote it. In the firſt place ſhe
cannot

cannot draw from them a revenue, until they are able to pay one, and when they are fo, they will be above fub-jection. Men foon become attached to the foil they live upon, and incorporated with the profperity of the place; and it fignifies but little what opinions they come over with, for time, intereft, and new connections will render them obfolete, and the next generation know nothing of them.

WERE Britain truly wife fhe would lay hold of the prefent opportunity to difentangle herfelf from all conti-nental embaraffments in North-America, and that not only to avoid future broils and troubles, but to fave ex-pences. For to fpeak explicitly on the matter, I would not, were I an European power, have Canada, under the conditions that Britain muft retain it, could it be given to me. It is one of thofe kind of dominions that is, and ever will be, a conftant charge upon any foreign holder.

As to Halifax, it will become ufelefs to England after the prefent war, and the lofs of the United States. A harbour, when the dominion is gone, for the purpofe of which only it was wanted, can be attended only with ex-pence. There are, I doubt not, thoufands of people in England, who fuppofe, that thofe places are a profit to the nation, whereas they are directly the contrary, and inftead of producing any revenue, a confiderable part of the revenue of England is annually drawn off, to fupport the expence of holding them.

GIBRALTAR is another inftance of national ill policy. A poft which in time of peace is not wanted, and in time of war is of no ufe, muft at all times be ufelefs. Inftead of affording protection to a navy, it requires the aid of one to maintain it. And to fuppofe that Gibraltar com-mands the Mediterranean, or the pafs into it, or the trade of it, is to fuppofe a detected falfhood; becaufe though Britain holds the poft, fhe has loft the other three, and every benefit fhe expected from it. And to fay that all this happens becaufe it is befieged by land and water, is to fay nothing, for this will always be the cafe in time of war, while France and Spain keep up fuperior fleets, and Britain holds the place.---So that, though as an impenetrable inacceffible rock it may be held by the one, it is always in the power of the other to render it ufelefs and exceffively chargeable.

K 2   I fhould

I fhould fuppofe that one of the principal objects of Spain in befieging it, is to fhow to Britain, that though fhe may not take it, fhe can command it, that is, fhe can fhut it up, and prevent its being ufed as a harbour, though not a garrifon.---But the fhort way to reduce Gibraltar, is, to attack the Britifh fleet; for Gibraltar is as dependent on a fleet for fupport, as a bird is on its wing for food, and when wounded there it ftarves.

There is another circumftance which the people of England have not only not attended to, but feem to be utterly ignorant of, and that is, the difference between permanent power, and accidental power, confidered in a national fenfe.

By permanent power, I mean, a natural inherent and perpetual ability in a nation, which though always in being, may not be always in action, or not always advantageoufly directed; and by accidental power, I mean, a fortunate or accidental difpofition or exercife of national ftrength, in whole or in part.

There undoubtedly was a time when any one European nation, with only eight or ten fhips of war, equal to the prefent fhips of the line, could have carried terror to all others, who had not began to build a navy, however great their natural ability might be for that purpofe: But this can be confidered only as accidental, and not as a ftandard to compare permanent power by, and could laft no longer than until thofe powers built as many or more fhips than the former. After this a larger fleet was neceffary, in order to be fuperior; and a ftill larger would again fuperfede it. And thus mankind have gone on building fleet upon fleet, as occafion or fituation dictated. And this reduces it to an original queftion, which is: Which power can build and man the largeft number of fhips? The natural anfwer to which, is, That power which has the largeft revenue and the greateft number of inhabitants, provided its fituation of coaft affords fufficient conveniencies.

France being a nation on the continent of Europe, and Britain an ifland in its neighbourhood, each of them derived different ideas from their different fituations. The inhabitants of Britain could carry on no foreign trade, nor ftir from the fpot they dwelt upon, without the affiftance of fhipping; but this was not the cafe with France. The idea therefore of a navy did not arife to

France

France from the fame original and immediate neceffity which produced it to England. But the queftion is, that when both of them turn their attention, and employ their revenues the fame way, which can be fuperior?

THE annual revenue of France is nearly double that of England, and her number of inhabitants more than twice as many. Each of them has the fame length of coaft on the channel, befides which, France has feveral hundred miles extent on the bay of Bifcay, and an opening on the Mediterranean: And every day proves that practice and exercife make failors as well as foldiers in one country as well as another.

IF then Britain can maintain an hundred fhips of the line, France can as well fupport an hundred and fifty, becaufe her revenues and her population are as equal to the one, as thofe of England are to the other. And the only reafon why fhe has not done it, is becaufe fhe has not till very lately attented to it. But when fhe fees, as fhe now fees, that a navy is the firft engine of power, fhe can eafily accomplifh it.

ENGLAND very falfely, and ruinoufly for herfelf, infer, that becaufe fhe had the advantage of France, while France had the fmaller navy, that for that reafon it is always to be fo. Whereas it may be clearly feen, that the ftrength of France has never yet been tried on a navy, and that fhe is able to be as fuperior to England in the extent of a navy, as fhe is in the extent of her revenues and her population. And England may lament the day, when, by her infolence and injuftice, fhe provoked in France a maritime difpofition.

IT is in the power of the combined fleets to conquer every ifland in the Weft-Indies, and reduce all the Britifh navy in thofe places. For were France and Spain to fend their whole naval force in Europe to thofe iflands, it would not be in the power of Britain to follow them with an equal force. She would ftill be twenty or thirty fhips inferior, were fhe to fend every veffel fhe had, and in the mean time all the foreign trade of England would lay expofed to the Dutch.

IT is a maxim, which, I am perfuaded, will ever hold good, and more efpecially in naval operations, that a great power ought never to move in detachments, if it can poffibly be avoided. But to go with its whole force to fome important object, the reduction of which fhall have

a

a decisive effect upon the war. Had the whole of the French and Spanish fleets in Europe come last spring to the West-Indies, every island had been their own, Rodney their prisoner, and his fleet their prize. From the United States the combined fleets can be supplied with provisions, without the necessity of drawing them from Europe, which is not the case with England.

ACCIDENT has thrown some advantages in the way of England, which, from the inferiority of her navy, she had not a right to expect. For though she has been obliged to fly before the combined fleets, yet Rodney has twice had the fortune to fall in with detached squadrons, to which he was superior in numbers: The first off Cape St. Vincent, where he had nearly two to one, and the other in the West-Indies, where he had a majority of six ships. Victories of this kind almost produce themselves. They are won without honor, and suffered without disgrace: And are ascribable to the chance of meeting, not to the superiority of fighting. For the same Admiral, under whom they were obtained, was unable, in three former engagements, to make the least impression on a fleet consisting of an equal number of ships with his own, and compounded for the events by declining the actions.*

To conclude, if it may be said that Britain has numerous enemies, it likewise proves that she has given numerous offences. Insolence is sure to provoke hatred, whether in a nation or an individual. The want of manners in the British Court may be seen even in its birthdays and new-years Odes, which are calculated to infatuate the vulgar, and disgust the man of refinement: And her former overbearing rudeness, and insufferable injustice on the seas, have made every commercial nation her foe. Her fleets were employed as engines of prey; and acted on the surface of the deep the character which the shark does beneath it.----On the other hand, the Combined Powers are taking a popular part, and will render their reputation immortal, by establishing the perfect freedom of the ocean, to which all countries have a right, and are interested in accomplishing. The sea is the world's highway; and he who arrogates a prerogative over it, transgresses

the

---

* See the accounts, either English or French, of three actions in the West-Indies, between Count de Guichen and Admiral Rodney, in 1780.

the right, and juftly brings on himfelf the chaftifement, of nations.

PERHAPS it might be of fome fervice to the future tranquility of mankind, were an article introduced into the next general peace, that no one nation fhould, in time of peace, exceed a certain number of fhips of war. Something of this kind feems neceffary; for according to the prefent fafhion, half the world will get upon the water, and there appears no end to the extent to which navies may be carried. Another reafon is, that navies add nothing to the manners or morals of a people. The fequeftered life which attends the fervice, prevents the opportunities of fociety, and is too apt to occafion a coarfenefs of ideas and language, and that more in fhips of war than in commercial employ; becaufe in the latter they mix more with the world, and are nearer related to it. I mention this remark as a general one; and not applied to any one country more than to another.

BRITAIN has now had the trial of above feven years, with an expence of nearly an hundred million pounds fterling; and every month in which fhe delays to conclude a peace, cofts her another million fterling, over and above her ordinary expences of government, which are a million more; fo that her total *monthly* expence is two million pounds fterling, which is equal to the whole *yearly* expence of America, all charges included. Judge then who is beft able to continue it.

SHE has likewife many atonements to make to an injured world, as well in one quarter as another. And inftead of purfuing that temper of arrogance, which ferves only to fink her in the efteem, and entail on her the diflike, of all nations, fhe would do well to reform her manners, retrench her expences, live peaceably with her neighbours, and think of war no more.

Philadelphia, Auguft 21, 1782.

E R R A T A.

Page 47, line 15, for principals read principles.
Page 60, line 17, for 1779 read 1778.

www.ingramcontent.com/pod-product-compliance
Lightning Source LLC
Chambersburg PA
CBHW020335090426
42735CB00009B/1548

* 9 7 8 3 3 3 7 1 0 5 8 0 8 *